Voice in the Wind

Jean D'Costa

Voice in the Wind

Longman Caribbean

LONGMAN CARIBBEAN LIMITED
TRINIDAD AND JAMAICA

Longman Group Limited
London

Associated companies, branches and representatives throughout the world

First published 1978

ISBN 0 582 76718 0

Printed in Hong Kong by
Wilture Enterprises (International) Ltd

To David

Preface

The story and characters of *Voice in the Wind* are fictional and bear no relationship to the deeds of persons living or dead. However the background of the story and some of the incidents mentioned in it are drawn from real life. There is a Virgin Valley farm near Somerton, but neither the house nor its occupants were such as I have described them. Nevertheless farm life on the small mixed farms of St. James and Trelawny was very much as it is presented here. The school, churches, bus service and cemetery of Somerton are based on my personal knowledge of that district, where I lived from 1942 until 1945. In presenting these background scenes from my childhood I wish to pay tribute to this district where I was very happy and which I will never forget.

Similarly, the house on Barnet Street is based on a real house, now much changed. The hospital is of course the old Montego Bay Hospital, known only too well to my family who were all treated there for such ailments as pneumonia and appendicitis. I well remember the humming of the wind along the corridors, and the noise of the sea was always there.

The only concrete fact which I have embedded in the story itself is the sinking of the *Freya*. Before starting on the novel I immersed myself in the newspapers of 1940–42, and so came across an account in the *Daily Gleaner* of March 1942 which described the torpedoeing and shelling of two Norwegian merchantmen. The account which Peter reads aloud to Dennis and Annabell is a verbatim statement of this episode of World War II.

Jean D'Costa
Golden Spring
St. Andrew
Jamaica

Chapter One

Shadow fell across the valley.

"A norther is coming: by tonight it'll be blowing hard." Mr Ferguson looked beyond the grey-green canefields to where dark hills marched up to the sky. "Have you got the lanterns and the lamps ready for tonight, Peter?"

"Why can't I do the lighting, Dad?" seven-year-old Dennis tugged at his father's khaki shirt. "Please Dad?"

Mr Ferguson ran down the steps of the low front verandah followed anxiously by all three children.

"I never get to do anything *nice*," complained Dennis. "Can't I light the lanterns, please?"

"Stop begging!" hissed Annabell. She was just ten and felt very old. "If you keep on bothering Dad you won't get to do a thing tonight. Let *me* ask."

Peter meanwhile was walking briskly down the drive with his father and going over for the dozenth time all the details of the black-out practice to be held that night in the district of Somerton. It was the last Saturday of January, 1941; the world war was more than a year old and air-raid practices had reached even the remotest villages of Jamaica. Somerton, by no means remote, lies some eight miles inland from the sea and prided itself even then on a Post Office, two shops, a Baptist Church beside the smart new Government School, a Presbyterian Church with a cemetery, a band that played once a month and a bus that went to

Montego Bay twice a week.

Mr Ferguson was on his way to catch that bus. He hoped to bring back tools for the farm and the monthly returns from the lawyer's office. He ran Virgin Valley farm for an old lawyer who lived in Kingston, and it was not always easy to meet all of the bills, especially in wartime.

"I won't light the Tilley lamp," promised Peter as they reached the turning of the main road. "It's the brightest one we've got, but I guess the warden will see the light of the other lamps anyway."

"Your mother may get home in time, of course," continued Mr Ferguson. "She'll light the Tilley lamp if she's home. Dennis and Annabell can light candles too, but those must be put out as soon as the signal is given."

Dennis pinched Annabell and made faces at her behind his father's back.

"The bus is coming! The bus is coming!" Annabell scrambled up the steep bank to escape from Dennis.

"Be good all of you! Remind Charlie to meet the bus tonight. I'll need help to carry everything up to the house."

He dropped a peck on Annabell's cheek, patted Dennis on the shoulder and waved to Peter who had decided on his last birthday that he was too old for that sort of thing. Peter would soon be twelve years old and drove his brother and sister mad by being nearly always right about everything from homework to guessing what their parents would say in any situation. This did not stop him from carrying out elaborate practical jokes, such as the time when he hid their dog Hitler under the platform of the Presbyterian Church where it howled an accompaniment to every hymn of a memorable Sunday School service. Or the dreadful Inspection Day when all of the chalk in the middle division of the school was found to be thoroughly soaked in black ink. Even Annabell wasn't sure if Peter had had anything to do with the chalk. He had been very shocked about it all, but at the time he was reading a large book called *Danny Dare, the Perfect Criminal.* He looked very thoughtful while the investigations were taking place, and he had so many helpful suggestions that Annabell was suspicious. But she wisely kept her thoughts to herself. It was well to keep in Peter's good books: who else would have rescued her when she got stuck in the ceiling of the Baptist Church that day when they were supposed to be helping to decorate it for Harvest Festival but searched for skeletons and treasure instead? And she could never get through the pasture where the bull was kept if Peter did not come along.

The bus swept off down the road in a cloud of white dust as the three children pelted back up the hill for a day of blissful freedom unspoilt by the interference of grown-ups. Even old Maud (who was usually on their side) was away at the doctor's over in Adelphi. Neither she nor their mother would be home until night. Leebert Hemmings, the Virgin Valley headman, might look in at midday if he wanted to leave a message for their father, and it was well to be careful with Leebert. He had a sensitive nose for mischief. Charlie, his son and right-hand man, was much more understanding.

"Race you up to the roof!" shouted Dennis as the three children dashed up the stony drive. He was last in every race but never gave up trying.

"No good now! Too cloudy! Won't see a thing!" sang out Peter, hopping lightly over the verandah railings. "Watch this you two!"

He leapt up to catch the beam above the railings and

raised himself in one smooth glide so that his chin rested on the beam. From there he surveyed them mockingly. The contrast between Peter and Dennis could not have been greater. Peter was tall for his age, thin as a wire and the colour of bitter chocolate. His black eyes had a way of laughing even when his face was still. Poor Dennis was as plump as a cushion. He hated being fat (except at mealtimes), but much, much more he hated his silky brown hair with its abominable curls and the grey-green eyes he had from their mother's side of the family. He would so much rather have looked like Annabell and Peter, alike as two peas in a pod, with their long swift legs, their black, tough hair and their eyes like glistening tar. Dennis was called *Puss-Eye* when he first went to school until Peter put a stop to it. But no one could stop the old ladies at church from stroking his hair and exclaiming over it. The three children thought them stupid.

"What about going to look for a good cave?" asked Peter, who was the self-appointed air-raid warden, intelligence officer, field marshal and air-force chief of Virgin Valley.

"Mamma won't let us," answered Annabell in a voice of gloom. "We're supposed to clean *all* of the shoes this morning and *then* do our homework."

"My shoes are quite clean–" began Dennis.

"Clean as mud, I bet!" broke in his sister rudely while Peter executed three magnificent cartwheels down the length of the verandah in between the tables and chairs.

"You be careful, Peter Ferguson!" warned Annabell. "You're supposed to behave well and set an example for the younger ones," she added in a perfect imitation of their father's voice.

Everybody burst out laughing and Peter said he supposed they had better go and clean all of the ugly old shoes first, and by then the sky might be clear and they could start the look-out for enemy ships at sea.

The house at Virgin Valley stood on one of the higher hills in the tumultuous range surrounding the farmlands. A gap in the mountains exposed them to the full force of the north wind in the winter months, but it also afforded a glimpse of the sea for any intrepid scout who might climb the roof of the old house. If one sat astride the cap of the roof, after a careful ascent with bare feet over gray shingles slippery with age, one would see to the north a small triangle of brilliant blue where shipping bound for Montego Bay usually passed. Peter had made this fascinating discovery quite by chance and lived in the hope of spotting a German destroyer or at least a battleship long before anyone else in Jamaica.

But the joys of war duty on the roof had to be carefully rationed. No one had actually forbidden the children to go up there, but their mother had shown a marked lack of enthusiasm for the scheme and would certainly have put a stop to Peter's war effort if she had known just what went on when she was safely out of the way. The children decided to carry out their special duty 'when no one was around to bother them,' as Peter put it.

"Today would be perfect," he sighed as he laboured over his father's second-best black shoes. "It had to go and be cloudy today of all days!"

"Maybe it'll clear up after lunch," Annabell added doubtfully. "That's if it doesn't rain. It looked just like this last Monday after Maud hung the washing out just before the thunderstorm. Everything got wet and she was mad as fire."

Dennis giggled. Both of his hands were plastered to the wrist with whitening but the crepe-soled shoes on the floor beside him looked little better for his trouble.

"I've done enough. I'm stopping now." Dennis announced this in a firm voice as Annabell stared pointedly at his handiwork. "Bet I beat you at dominoes, Peter!"

This wild challenge was treated with the scorn it deserved and by the time Annabell had gone off to fetch the lemonade and egg sandwiches left for them by their mother, Peter was several games to the good and had forgotten the clouds in the sky. The early afternoon was spent pleasantly enough down in the small pasture behind the house where three ancient tombstones made a sun-baked platform for reading, drawing or just dozing out-of-doors. The bull who lived in the pasture was away on loan to a distant farm, so Annabell was free to roam in search of the many-coloured four o'clocks in bloom all through the field.

By mid-afternoon the wind began to rise as Mr Ferguson had foreseen. It blew with a steady cold force from the north, breaking up the cloud bank and moaning in the cedar trees above the tombstones.

"It's too cold to sit out here and read." Annabell shut her book with a snap and jumped down. "Just listen to the wind!"

Dennis mumbled something and went on reading, but Peter glanced up. He was sitting on the highest of the old brick tombs; the children had played around them ever since they were tiny and felt that nothing so old could possibly be menacing. The cemetery by the church was another matter. Peter said he was not afraid to walk across it alone on a dark night, but Annabell and Dennis were not too sure. But these tombs were so old and moss-grown that you could hardly read the inscriptions on the worn marble. The largest and highest was the tomb of one Ezekiel Martin Esq., of this Parish, who died June 3rd, 1776. As for the others, the children neither knew nor cared.

"It's *cold*!" repeated Annabell. "I'm going back. I've got to finish my homework and start supper."

"What? Supper?" Dennis sat up with a jerk.

"Thought that would wake you up," said his sister sarcastically. "It isn't ready. You can come and help me too. Mamma said both of you should help."

Very soon all three children were hurrying between the old-fashioned brick-paved kitchen where Mistress Maud ruled with an iron hand, and the crowded little pantry which opened off the passage at the back of the house. They were careful as they went in and out of the kitchen: it was far more dangerous to leave the kitchen untidy than to spill jam on the tablecloth in the dining room. So Peter, in charge of roasting breadfruit, set up a small coalpot in a corner of the backyard and left both the gleaming Dover stove and the stone fireplace untouched. Dennis juiced oranges in the pantry while Annabell sliced tomatoes and opened a large tin of bully beef. She made Dennis tidy away all of the orange peel before they laid the table.

"And homework before supper!" It was one of their mother's favourite warnings and even if Annabell was showing off by sounding just like her, Dennis went with dragging feet and only one or two backward glances at the dining table to fetch his schoolbag from the shelf where he had crammed it on Friday afternoon. Peter needed no reminder, for he was working for a scholarship examination later that year. The thought of *not* going to Cornwall College in a year's time was enough to stop his breath for a moment and drive every other thought from his head.

Annabell tried and tried to concentrate on the poem she was learning by heart. The wind was growing stronger and now was working at every loose shutter and ill-fitting door in the old house.

"Just listen to that!" she exclaimed as a shrill whistle ended with a loud bang upstairs.

Peter was lost in arithmetic and only Dennis looked up, wide-eyed. Outside the grey sky grew darker; soon it would be too dark to see.

"It – it sounds just like people talking upstairs–" Annabell peeped through the window at the driveway now dim and pale under the wind-tossed trees. "Do – do you think Mamma will be home soon?"

Dennis shivered and hugged his reading book closer to his chest. Annabell shivered too and wondered if she should take the long journey down the dark passage, up the stairs and along the corridor to her room where her sweater was hanging on a peg in the closet. It suddenly seemed a long way to go alone.

"Peter? If you're going upstairs would you bring my sweater? It's in the closet."

"What? Go and get it yourself. Don't you see I'm busy? I've got to finish this now for we can't light the lamp until the bell rings. Take Dennis if you're scared, or Hitler."

He returned to his arithmetic and Dennis suddenly became absorbed in his spelling book. Annabell sighed.

The passage was not as dark as she had feared, but the wind did howl so sadly in the trees outside. A hundred draughts went shrilling and muttering from every corner of the house.

The stairs creaked crossly as she stepped on them. For

some reason she could not hurry but went up step by slow step instead of two at a time.

"The others should see me now!" she thought as she went gliding along the corridor. "I am a great queen going all alone to the secret temple where I will save my people."

She opened the closet.

"My robes, scarlet and silver, with a crown of silver lace like net and one white diamond on my forehead." The Queen slid into the old blue sweater knitted two years ago by Mamma and getting short in the sleeve now.

"I'll walk all alone through the pitch-dark temple up to the high altar and –"

The wind rose to a high shriek all too human in its piercing wail. The Queen started violently and slammed the closet door. Annabell returned to earth with a jolt and stood stock-still gripping the sweater round her shoulders. For a long moment everything was still. The creakings and groanings of the house stopped. The tops of the trees outside were motionless. The wind held its breath. Then, suddenly as it stopped, the gale sprang into life and whipped across the trees.

Annabell jumped again. In the racing wind came a ripple of laughter. Unmistakable laughter. Real laughter.

A flash of anger shot through her. It must be Peter and Dennis trying to frighten her. Well, they'd soon see, the mean wretches!

She tiptoed to the door and listened.

Nothing.

The passage and the stairs were silent, and there at the table in the drawing room were Peter and Dennis poring over their books in the last light of day. She stood unnoticed in the darkening doorway and watched them.

"Oh! There you are! Did you get lost?" Peter pushed aside his books and got up. "What's wrong with you?"

Annabell looked at him hard. Peter was an accomplished actor, but the ink on his exercise book was still wet.

"Can we have supper now? Before it's too dark to see?" broke in Dennis.

"What were you two laughing at just now?" Annabell's face was serious.

"We weren't laughing at anything. We weren't even talking." Peter stared at her. "You heard something?"

Annabell nodded.

"Maybe Charlie's here." Peter jumped up.

"No-o." Annabell did not move. "It sounded like one of you, or maybe like Mamma. It wasn't a man, and it couldn't be Maud."

"Well it must be a duppy," began Dennis even though he got scared of the dark far more easily than either of the others.

"Rubbish. Let's go and see if anybody is coming up the drive." Peter began packing his books away in a shabby red schoolbag.

"Somebody *is* coming!" shouted Dennis from the window. "A car is coming! It must be Uncle Edwin!"

Homework, supper and duppies forgotten, the three children rushed through the door, pounded along the verandah and plunged down the steps.

"That's not Uncle Edwin!" yelled Peter. "It's Uncle Simon Peter!"

His voice rose above the shrieking wind and the growl of the Austin Seven labouring up the hill. The tiny car was moving at a crawl. Peter and Annabell mounted the back bumper with practised skill while

Dennis puffed alongside.

Up through the gates hastily opened by Dennis went the car, toiling more slowly under its extra burden. It shuddered to a stop level with the verandah steps and the driver's door swung open.

A pair of giant arms seized first Annabell and then Dennis. A bristly kiss was planted on Annabell's cheek; mingled in the air where the scent of bay rum and rich tobacco as Great Uncle Simon Peter climbed stiffly out of the little black car.

In the gathering dark he towered above them.

His small hand lost in the great fist that clasped his firmly, Dennis looked up and thought again that Great Uncle Simon Peter was the very biggest person he had ever seen. Perhaps he was still growing; Dennis decided to ask the others what they thought.

"Let me look at you! Dennis, your head almost passes the buckle of my belt! But why is all in darkness?"

Three voices began to explain and to ask questions at once.

"One by one!" Uncle Simon Peter lumbered heavily across the verandah and lowered himself into the largest of the heavy wooden verandah chairs. His white hair and beard glowed silver in the twilight.

"When did the *Freya* reach port?"

"Would you like some supper *now,* Uncle Simon Peter?"

"What did you bring us this time, Uncle Simon Peter?"

"Did you see lots of battleships and submarines, sir?"

"Do you want to wait until Mamma and Dad come home?"

"Uncle Simon Peter, may we go and look at the *Freya* this time? You promised us, remember?"

"Wait! Wait! My poor ears! One by one, now. But first tell me why I see no lights anywhere. Is Jamaica now becoming as perilous as England and my poor Norway?"

"We're having black-out practice tonight," explained Peter. "We have to get used to doing things in the dark, and showing no lights that could be seen out at sea –"

"And then the church bells will ring and everybody will light their lamps," broke in Dennis. "Annabell and I will light candles–"

"The warden is looking out now," Peter went on, "and anybody who shows a light after dark will get in trouble. Until the bells ring, of course."

"Peter will light our lamps," added Annabell. "We've got everything ready."

Uncle Simon Peter was silent for a moment.

Peter could see his godfather's face dimly, but he looked pale, tired and worried. How could he be really worried? The *Freya* was a sound little merchant vessel which travelled in the armed convoy across the Atlantic. For the first time since the war began an edge of something like fear touched Peter as he looked up into the old captain's face. There was war in Norway, the captain's former home. Dad had told them about quislings, spies, traitors and the invading Nazi armies. Uncle Simon Peter would say very little except that the third mate, Andersen, had gone off to join a Resistance group and had not been heard from since.

Dennis climbed into Uncle Simon Peter's lap.

"Dad went to Montego Bay today. He's coming home on the bus tonight," he began chattily.

"Ah! I did not stop in Montego Bay, not even at the house on Barnet Street." Uncle Simon Peter's voice was deep and slow. A rich voice, thought Annabell, like fruit cake and woodsmoke and Maud's roast beef gravy. Suddenly the memory of the laughing voice in the wind came unbidden to her mind. Who could it have been? Perhaps the noises of the wind had made her imagine things; there it was now playing with the curtains, ruffling the sheet music on the piano and tinkling the beaded fringe of the lampshade. Annabell loved that tall silk lampshade with its rippling fringe. It covered the globe of the high brass lamp that came from Barnet Street where two others just like it stood in Great Aunt Flossie's drawing room. Great Uncle Simon Peter had bought them, and Aunt Flossie had made the shades of pleated gold silk and threaded the glittering fringes the year before she died. That was long ago, when Dennis was only one year old, but Annabell could remember playing with the cascades of shining beads while someone smelling of lavender water held her up to reach the shade as the clear sounds chimed together. Uncle Simon Peter's voice recalled her wandering thoughts.

"Yes, Uncle Simon Peter? A glass of sorrel? Oh yes! Mamma made lots for Christmas, and Maud made some pimento dram for you too."

While Annabell searched carefully in the dark pantry for glasses and a jug, Dennis and Peter dragged chairs close up to Uncle Simon Peter and waited impatiently for answers to their questions.

Yes, London had been bombed; the docks too, but not in the three days when the *Freya* was unloading at the Royal Albert docks. They had seen the glow of fires to the west when they were anchored off the mouth of the Thames at night, waiting for the convoy which would escort them across the Atlantic. There were battleships and destroyers in the Channel but no, Uncle Simon

Peter had seen no yerman ships close at hand. Dennis stifled a giggle. Even after twenty years of marriage to Great Aunt Flossie and nearly forty of plying between London and Montego Bay, Uncle Simon Peter still said 'y' for 'j' in a strong Norwegian accent.

"What about tanks? Did you see any in London?" Peter was eager for news and read all the war magazines avidly. "And armoured cars?"

"No. Yust lots of soldiers and sailors and men in the R.A.F. You won't see tanks save at the docks where they ship them overseas. And at the front, of course. At the front." He was silent again. "When did this black-out practice start, Peter?"

"Tonight's the first night," broke in Dennis. "You can help us if you like," he added generously.

Uncle Simon Peter took the tall glass that Annabell brought to him on a small tray.

"Ah! That is good! I wish I had known your father was in Montego Bay today. We could have come home together. You are all the home I have now that Florence is gone. You and the old *Freya*."

The children did not know what to say. Uncle Simon Peter occasionally said things like that. Dennis supposed it was because he was so very, very old: sixty-five at least, Dad said. Even Maud wasn't as old as that. He wondered what it felt like to be so old, and if he too would have a white beard and whiskery moustache in the unlikely event that he grew as old as that. Then he gave up trying to work it out as a more pressing thought occurred to him.

"Didn't you bring us something this time, Uncle Simon Peter?" he asked anxiously. "I've got something put up for you since *Christmas*. Or, well, Mamma put it up and I can't find it without the lamp."

Uncle Simon Peter laughed.

"Do you think I cross the sea only to bring you presents, Master Parrot? We will all have to wait until the lamps can be lit, and then we will see."

Chapter Two

Uncle Simon Peter was just setting down his empty glass when the faint sound of footsteps crunching on the gravelled drive announced the arrival of Maud and Mrs Ferguson. There were hugs and handshakes and exclamations of 'De good Lawd bless you!" In Maud's eyes Uncle Simon Peter was a revered and important person, second only to the memory of her dead Missis. The children's mother she regarded affectionately as a Christian young lady, coming up nicely, while she looked upon their father and Uncle Edwin as two small boys in need of firm discipline and guidance. Peter, Annabell and Dennis were small fry to be scolded or spoiled as the spirit moved her.

"What a nuisance this blackout is!" Mrs Ferguson started to bustle about, or to try to in spite of the dimness of the verandah and the pitch dark inside the house. "You must all be starving! Did you lay the table Annabell? And did you all finish your homework? And the evenings are so short at this time of year!"

"It's all ready, Mamma. We got everything done in time. Couldn't we have supper out here, in the dark?" asked Annabell.

"We could if we knew where everything was,"

answered her mother. "But somebody is sure to knock over a glass or two, and I don't fancy eating a moth or an ant by mistake!"

Everybody laughed and Uncle Simon Peter said they had better wait for the black-out to end. Mrs Ferguson brought out the jug of orange juice and some biscuits so that Dennis was saved from immediate starvation and Maud's bad stomach kept the peace with her.

The wind was as strong as ever, but now the sky had cleared and a faint starlight brought out the lines of road, trees and white verandah railings where the darker shapes of Uncle Simon Peter, Mrs Ferguson and Maud showed against the pale backdrop of canefields stretching away below the house.

Uncle Simon Peter drew out his watch at Dennis' insistence and announced that the time was a quarter to eight.

"How can you see that, Uncle Simon Peter?" Dennis screwed up his eyes to read the phosphorescent dial. To tell the truth, he wasn't always sure how to read a clock even in daylight: the long and short hands did such peculiar things.

"As late as that! You children should be getting ready for bed!" exclaimed Mrs Ferguson.

A chorus of protests met this remark.

"Well, tonight *is* different, so you may stay up a while after supper, but don't forget you're all going to church in the morning!"

"Will you come with us, Uncle Simon Peter?" begged Annabell. The rare appearances of their great uncle at the Presbyterian church in Somerton were always something in the nature of a sensation. Since the outbreak of war he had become even more of a personage, while the spectacle of Dennis sharing a hymnbook with a large man who stood six foot three was enough to bring a thin smile to the lips of Parson Hay. The children in Dennis's Sunday School class gazed on him with open mouths, and Maud said that you didn't need the organ when Captain led the singing.

"Now children, your uncle is very tired. Don't torment him and don't expect him to go with you. They'll only keep him there for hours giving all the news of the world!"

"No Annabell," Uncle Simon Peter replied, "not tomorrow. I cannot stay long anymore; not in war time. The *Freya* must sail at dawn on Tuesday if we are to meet the convoy. I have to leave you in the morning."

There was a longer pause as everyone digested this.

"Suppose – suppose you miss the convoy, Uncle Simon Peter?" asked Dennis. Annabell was silent. She hated everything to do with the war, and used to get furious with Peter if she found any of his drawings of bombers and tanks in her painting book.

"Well, I can put into an American port and wait for another," explained Uncle Simon Peter. "But that would make the *Freya* late. While the weather at least is good we must make all speed. Herr Hitler does not wait on anyone."

Against her will Mrs Ferguson said, "It *is* getting very bad, isn't it? The newspapers are bad enough but the rumours are worse!"

"Is de work of de Devil, pure an' simple," came Maud's voice from the rocking chair in the corner. "If Missis was livin' today she would explain it to all a you. De Bible warn us dat all dis mus' take place before de End. Mek Missa 'Itler carry on, tink say him so wonderful. All 'im good for is fi do Satan work." She cackled with laughter. "Wait till 'im see Satan wages what 'im work so hard for!"

Suddenly Annabell sat up straight.

"The bells! The bells are ringing!"

"Come on Peter!" yelled Dennis.

The children leaped to their feet as the cold bright tolling of a bell came to them across the shadowy hills and valleys.

"What've you done with the matches? Don't tell me you've lost them!" cried Annabell as Peter hunted in his pockets.

A match flared and showed Peter's face in its golden light as he lit the first lamp and brought it out on to the verandah.

"Bring the candles and the other lamps, you idiots!" he shouted after his brother and sister.

"An' jus' look at dat, Miss Peggy!" exclaimed Maud as she and Mrs Ferguson turned towards the rolling hills of Somerton. One by one, two by two, red and golden lights sparked alive in the darkness, some below them along the main road leading to Crossroads, others high up in the hills south and east over towards the direction of Cedar Hill. One shone with a piercing white light at the head of the valley.

"That must be up on the hill at the old manse! Teacher Creary has lit the new gas lamp! Look, you can even make out the windows from here!"

But Maud was wiping her spectacles and muttering about the chilliness of the evening.

"All a you mus' be well hungry. Come on, Miss Peggy: please can bring in de Captain an' set roun' de table. An' all you children go wash you hands an' come!"

The Tilley lamp lit, Maud and Mrs Ferguson were

busy in the pantry where salt fish fritters and a large omelette were added to the dishes on the table. In the midst of all this Mr Ferguson and Charlie arrived, and Uncle Simon Peter took them out to the car to unload a heavy wooden box which they took into the drawing room despite Mrs Ferguson's protests.

The lamps shone bright as they sat down to supper around the table. War shortages had not yet reduced food supplies to a serious level, and in any case Jamaica never experienced the severe rationing known in England and war-time Europe. Butter was short, and all tinned food, but Mr Ferguson had brought salted shrimp from Montego Bay which went very well with the roasted breadfruit, fried yam and fresh bread from a famous bakery in Montego Bay. Maud's banana pone filled all remaining corners, and the children grudgingly drank a glass of milk each while the grown-ups had tea.

Clearing up was accomplished with amazing speed: the boys had to help, too. All three children knew that only when Mamma and Maud were satisfied would they be allowed back in the drawing room where the mysterious wooden crate was even then being wrenched open by their father.

"I got the bearings for you, and all of the other parts on your list," rumbled Uncle Simon Peter's deep voice. A heavy smell of machine oil hung in the air and Peter entered the room to see his father peering at what looked like the block of an engine. Annabell wrinkled her nose as she came in behind him.

"Is that the new pump, Dad?" Peter loved machines. He alone could repair his mother's Singer sewing machine when the bobbin jammed, and he would have stripped it down every week if allowed.

"Yes, this is for the new pump," Mr Ferguson was

saying. "We have to get more water out of the spring this year. A bad drought will finish us."

Annabell thought that her father looked as tired as Uncle Simon Peter. He was a tall man too, and their shadows flung a great bear-like shape on the wall behind them.

"And now you, my children!" Uncle Simon Peter's eyes shot a sudden, piercing glance at the three eager faces looking up at him.

Out of the depths of the crate came a plain cardboard box. Not much to look at, but Annabell's heart pounded. Dennis held his breath as Peter took the oddly heavy box and laid it on the table by the lamp.

"Hurry up Peter! Open it quick!" Dennis made a futile grab at the box.

For once Annabell said nothing. Uncle Simon Peter never remembered birthdays and was seldom home for Christmas, but the presents which he brought at odd times you treasured forever. There were the six tiny Japanese dolls in brightly coloured silks lying in their case by her bed. Peter was never without the Scout knife with its four blades, screwdriver, file and tiny scissors. In Dennis's cupboard were the precious remains of a musical top he had had for years, and as for the fantastic garlands and glass ornaments which they hung on the Christmas tree each year, or the brilliant Chinese lanterns of crimson, emerald and iridescent blue, those were good enough for Aladdin's cave or a banquet on the moon, thought Annabell.

But this time the presents looked disappointing. All that she could see inside the box were three smaller boxes packed in straw. Two were very small and were labelled 'Annabell' and 'Dennis' in rather spidery handwriting.

"Good things come in small parcels, your Great Aunt used to say." Uncle Simon Peter smiled at her under bushy brows as if he had read her thoughts.

Slowly she stretched out her hand and took the little blue box from Peter. Dennis was already struggling to undo the neat hard knots around the tiny red box, smallest of the three, while Peter was unwrapping rolls of brown paper from his parcel.

Peter was the first to finish.

He choked out,

"Binoculars! *Real* proper binoculars! *Gosh!* Wait till I show those boys at school!" then, remembering his manners, "Thank you *so* much, Uncle Simon Peter! They're *great!*"

"For your war work, you know. A look-out must have his glasses." Uncle Simon Peter's eyes danced and Peter wondered how it was that he always knew what was going on even though he hardly ever spent as much as a week on shore.

"And what about you two?" Uncle Simon Peter glanced at Dennis labouring to cut the string with a pair of embroidery scissors borrowed from his mother.

Annabell's reluctant fingers found the latch of the blue case just as Dennis cut through the last cord.

Dennis gasped and jumped to his feet but Annabell could not find her voice.

"Your compass! You've given me your compass!"

A tiny brass compass, its face no more than an inch wide, gleamed in Dennis's hand.

"So you will find your way home, even in war." Dennis almost disappeared in a vast hug. "I have had that compass since I was a boy, hardly as old then as you are now. But do you not like your present, my Annabell?"

"Do – do you really want me to keep this, Uncle

Simon Peter?" her voice sounded strange in her own ears. Very carefully she lifted up the long silver chain with its curiously wrought links from which swung a silver ladies' watch, Great Aunt Flossie's watch with its lid engraved with rose shapes and the flowing letters S.P.N. to F.A.R. worked on the inside of the lid.

"Give it to your mother to put away," began Mr Ferguson as Uncle Simon Peter undid the clasp and hung the chain about Annabell's neck.

"No, no, Yoe. My Annabell will keep it safe, I know. These are for you to have now –" he paused as if he had meant to say more and changed his mind suddenly.

Mrs Ferguson was quite as shocked as Annabell herself but all she said to the children was to be sure not to lose the boxes and to promise never to take them to school or to lend them to anyone.

"Don't worry, Joe," she smiled at Mr Ferguson's worried face. "They'll take good care of them."

On the way up to bed Dennis made the pleasing discovery that the dial of the compass could be read in the dark just like Uncle Simon Peter's watch. Of course the silver watch had to be carefully scrutinised and was found to be phosphorescent too. Annabell suddenly ran downstairs and kissed Uncle Simon Peter again.

"What's got into her?" asked Dennis, spreading toothpaste on his brush with a lavish hand.

But he fell asleep that night with the brass compass close beside him on the bedside table, its ghostly needle pointing due north to the darkened seas; Annabell slept with the silver chain coiled round her wrist, its strangely shaped figures glinting in the half-dark and the watch clasped tightly in her hand.

Chapter Three

Next morning was bright and cold as it so often is when the norther is blowing from the wintry expanse of north America. But even Dennis was up early despite the chill, and there was less grumbling than usual in the bathroom. Uncle Simon Peter's visits tended to have that effect on the children.

"I think it's a wicked shame that he's got to leave again so soon!" whispered Annabell to Peter as they made their way downstairs. "I bet he doesn't want to leave today!"

"But he's *got* to. Don't you understand anything about the war?" began Peter in a rather superior voice.

"Hey! Wait for me, you two!" Dennis came tumbling down the stairs making a lot of noise and causing Annabell to frown at him.

"Good morning Miss Fuss-an'-Feathers! Who're you looking at like that? Everybody got up ages ago. Mamma and Maud are out in the garden, and Dad's taken Uncle Simon Peter to look at the place where he's putting in the new pump. So yah-yah-yaah!"

"The new pump!" exclaimed Peter, pushing Dennis out of his way. Before Annabell could say another word both boys were through the backdoor and across the yard in a flash.

Annabell made her way slowly to the pantry, her mind in a tangle of thoughts: the war, and Aunt Flossie's watch, and Uncle Simon Peter leaving so soon, and getting ready for church and wondering if she would remember that poem on Monday morning in class.

Maud's voice coming from the direction of the flower garden interrupted her thoughts.

"Come help me fix up de flowers dem for Captain to put on Missis grave. Come, chile." Maud was standing near the verandah railing, her arms full of white tuberoses, lilies and Queen Anne's lace. "Here! Take dem from me."

With much puffing and blowing Maud ascended the four shallow steps of the verandah.

"Bring dem come into de pantry an' pass me dat ole paint tin fi put dem in. Captain will 'ave to put dem in de vase but dem mus' travel safe into somet'ing what not goin' to break or turn over in de car."

So Annabell, jealously watched by Maud, put first pebbles and then sand into the gallon tin; then she arranged the flowers carefully so as not to damage the stems on the trip to town.

"Now bring some water in de goblet," instructed Maud, taking the tin away from Annabell. "Captain always 'ave good t'ings for Missis. She keeping a place for 'im right 'gainst 'arself in Parish Church yard. Is only dat 'im time don' come as yet. Don't t'row 'way de water on me clean, clean floor! Lawd 'ave mercy! Is where you Muma get dis baff-'and pickney from?"

She snatched the enamel jug from Annabell, muttering to herself. Her glasses slid down to the end of her nose and the starched ends of her tall red head-tie quivered as she bent over the flowers.

"Alright, now." She stood back and admired her handiwork. "It favour somet'ing decent. Carry it outside an' give Captain. Take time an' don' drap it!"

Annabell and the others never argued with Maud,

because she was very kind and only pretended to be cross.

After a spanking or a scold, it was in Maud's kitchen (an area zealously guarded from all other grown-ups) that Peter would find congenial silence and coconut drops. Dennis would have spent his whole life in there if allowed, though it must be admitted that this was partly because of his keen personal interest in all that went on in the kitchen. Annabell liked best the stories Maud told about times long ago, when she was a girl in Vaughansfield, and rolling-calves and headless ladies patrolled the cross-roads at night. But best of all was the rare privilege of sitting on the edge of Maud's brass bed, left her by no less a person than Great Aunt Flossie herself, with its queer shining knobs, sockets, and end-pieces that you could unscrew, and its patch-work quilt made by Maud with the sky-blue linen patch that was Aunt Flossie's best dress when she started the boarding-house, and the green striped cotton that she made her aprons from, and a bit and piece of every single dress she had made for customers in the hard, long years between the death of Great Uncle Josiah and Uncle Simon Peter's courtship. But those occasions were few and far between; Maud had little time for stories, and nowadays she had to stop and gasp for breath if she tried to walk up the hill in one go. Mrs Ferguson had managed to stop her washing up the plates and pots, a task now shared by Charlie and the children. But no other hand could dust the furniture or do the fine starching and ironing, though she grudgingly allowed Leebert's cousin Ivy to do the heavy cleaning and the Monday wash.

Maud went out to the verandah to watch Annabell put the flowers in the car, she said, but in truth she wanted a last good look at Uncle Simon Peter before he left. Every time it was the same; she would look at him and say she was not getting younger and take off her glasses to wipe her eyes. Uncle Simon Peter would put a great paw on her shoulder and laugh, and say he was sure she would be married by the time he came back again. Then everybody would laugh, Maud louder than the rest, and she would shuffle back into the house saying she had work to do before night.

Her spectacles were starting to mist over as Uncle Simon Peter was hugged and kissed and told a hundred things by five different voices. He turned to Maud, but this time she stood far away from him in the shade of the verandah, shaking her head and saying nothing.

"You don't want to say goodbye to me, Miss Maud?" Uncle Simon Peter asked, looking at her over the children's heads. But she did not move towards him. Her lips worked, and she began to raise her hand as if to beckon to him, but instead she turned suddenly and hurried into the house.

Annabell thought it queer, and Peter and Dennis both stared at the door where Maud had disappeared.

"Let me go and say–" Uncle Simon Peter began, setting down his pipe.

"No, no. Best let her be." Mrs Ferguson broke in quickly. "She's not feeling well this morning; just let her alone for now. I'll talk to her a little later."

The children wondered what was wrong with Maud, and if the doctor would have to be sent for from Adelphi. But their mother was busy arranging parcels and boxes in the car, calling at the same time to Peter to hold the tin of flowers and to Dennis to run and fetch the ball of string from the pantry. They soon forgot about Maud's odd behaviour, dismissing it as just one of the many dull mysteries that grown-ups spend so much time fussing and whispering about behind closed doors. They ran all the way down the drive and out on to the road, keeping pace with the spluttering Austin Seven.

After that the day seemed very flat. They did not go to Sunday School, and even Peter said that that would be better than sitting around at home now that Uncle Simon Peter had gone. Lunch was a poor affair of cow-foot stew, rice-and-pumpkin, with spinach, which even Dennis loathed. They were sent upstairs to rest after lunch, which really meant that their parents wanted a nap.

As soon as the house was quiet, Annabell crept out of her little bedroom at the head of the stairs, and went like a shadow to the boys' room across the landing. Dennis was sitting on the floor doing a jigsaw puzzle, and Peter was hanging out of the window studying the cane-fields with the binoculars. It was difficult to converse, because their parents' bedroom was next to that room. Annabell found an end of chalk in the snarled mess of the top drawer of the chest of drawers, and wrote SPARE ROOM on the floor beside Dennis. She rubbed it out thoroughly and the boys nodded.

They had to get down on hands and knees and creep very, very carefully past the half-open door to their parents' room. If they stood up, they would be reflected in the long mirror of the mahogany wardrobe just inside the doorway. But Peter and Annabell had once discovered that if you lay almost flat, you could wriggle along below the level of the mirror. The high polish on the floor helped a lot, though it was inclined to leave a tell-tale stain on one's clothes. Dennis did not do it as well as the others, but they had made him practise the whole manoeuvre several times until he could manage at least to get by without making a noise.

As soon as they were safely in the spare room, where a smell of pipe tobacco and bay rum still lingered, Peter said,

"Let's go on the roof!"

The other two stared at him.

"You must be mad!" exclaimed Annabell. "With Dad and Mamma at home, and on a Sunday afternoon! Not even Maud would let us! We *can't!*"

Peter looked mulish. He had the binoculars in his hand, and of course he wanted nothing better than to look out to sea with them. The afternoon was passing, and every moment seemed a terrible waste.

"Oh we can get up there without any noise," he said airily. "Well, *I* can. The two of you can stay here. You don't have to come, any way. I don't think you better come with me after all."

He picked up the binoculars, looking very superior, and prepared to slip out of the back door on to the balcony. Both Annabell and Dennis launched themselves on him at once. The ensuing fight was short and fierce, conducted in grim silence with every nerve strained to catch the least noise from their parents' room. Annabell hung on to the binoculars and received a terrible twist to her arm. Dennis was sent flying with a blow to the chest that landed him in the middle of the bed. It is a wonder that no one heard them.

The next moment Peter had pushed the binoculars into his shirt, and was out on the landing. As he began climbing Annabell was much tempted to slam the window shut, so that he would have nothing to hold on to, and nowhere to put his feet. But her arm ached too much, and suddenly in her mind's eye she saw a quick, tiny picture of Peter slipping from the window, rolling across the verandah roof, and falling on the stone steps below. So she pressed her face to the jalousies instead and whispered as loud as she dared,

"Very good, Mr Peel-neck Porcupine! I hope you stay up there for the rest of your life!"

They could hear him treading softly across the roof above them; then silence. After a short while Annabell whispered to Dennis that she was going back to her room, and he might as well do the same. So Dennis went back to his jigsaw puzzle of elephants marching through the jungle, and Annabell took *Jack O'Lantern*, a favourite story of Peter's, and one which she had already read three times, and settled down in her room to make the best of a bad bargain. Now and then both Dennis and Annabell thought how mean Peter was, and Annabell made up a string of names like Johncrow Parson, Wirefoot and Lizardmouth to call him at the earliest suitable opportunity. But they did not betray him.

So it was that about half an hour later, when Annabell was deep in the adventures of Jack O'Lantern and a group of French refugees snatched from Madame Guillotine and the Reign of Terror, she was startled to hear a heavy thump-thump-thump on the roof above. She and Dennis peeped into the passage at the same time, Dennis's eyes like saucers. She pressed her finger to her lips and frowned hard at him to be quiet. The next minute they could both hear the sound of feet on the roof, followed by a scrabbling noise and a very distinct grunt. They dived back into their respective rooms in a hurry at the sound of their father's voice at the end of the passage, followed by the dreadful and unmistakable noises of their parents getting out of bed.

"What's that on the roof?" It was Mamma, in her

dressing gown, hurrying out in the passage. "Peter! Annabell!"

"Yes, Mamma?" Annabell sat up in bed, so that her mother was obliged to stop and look in at the door to answer her. This gave Peter an extra fraction of a minute to climb down while his mother's back was turned to the door at the other end of the passage.

"Did you hear that noise on the roof just now?" Mrs Ferguson paused only for a moment. "It sounds like someone climbing on the roof." She turned to look towards the boys' room.

At that moment Peter, who was having trouble holding on to the binoculars and the jalousies at the same time, decided to save the binoculars from falling, and jumped down to the verandah roof with a heavy thud. It was a great jump; many times after that, he described the awful moment to Annabell and Dennis, and showed them how high up he was when he jumped.

Of course that did it.

"Good gracious heavens!" ejaculated Mrs Ferguson, running to the end of the passage in the direction of the noise. "Joe! Joe! Come at once!"

But Mr Ferguson was up and out beside her even before she called him. Annabell and Dennis exchanged worried glances across the passage and stayed prudently where they were. Nothing they did now could help the wretched Peter, and perhaps, if they were seen to be innocent, the precious binoculars might not be confiscated altogether. But it was a desperate hope. It would be alleged that none of them was responsible enough to keep such a valuable gift, and that it was plainly leading them into temptation. As for going up on the roof with it–! And during Sunday rest–! Annabell turned cold at the thought.

But as she strained her ears for the first sounds of the inevitable punishment, she heard instead shouts from Peter, a muffled cry from her father, then feet running down the backstairs, and her mother calling "Maud! Maud! Annabell and Dennis! Come quickly! Come at once!"

Dennis almost knocked her over as they rushed down the passage together in time to see their father and Peter running across the backyard to the nearest paddock.

"What's happening, Mamma," began Annabell. But she did not need an answer. They were all facing the window, and they all could see down to the foot of the hill where a thin column of blue smoke rose from the cane-fields, burning swiftly in the dry, clear air.

Mrs Ferguson seized them both by the hand and hurried them down the stairs.

"Thank God you're dressed!" she gasped. "Take the short cut, the two of you, go and tell Leebert! Ask him to come up with Charlie and all the men he can find! Hurry! Tell them to bring machetes! Remember that! And buckets! No, wait. Stay with me here, Dennis. I'll need you." Annabell paused only to kick off her shoes. She could run like the wind straight down the steepest hill, clinging with bare feet to smooth rocks and clumps of grass, flinging herself downwards so that her feet flashed sideways across the slope to keep her balance. She was through the back paddock in seconds, past the three tombstones, forgetting the bull, who would have had a hard time catching her if he had been there. Down the steep slope she ran where the guavas grow among patches of cow-itch, devil's-horse-whip, four-o'clocks and black-eye-susan. She fell once. Afterwards her legs were covered with weals from cow-itch, her hands were cut, and her clothes so full of burrs that Mrs Ferguson almost threw them away in despair. She felt strangely small and light, as though she had no weight but strength to burst through anything in her way. And she felt nothing at all when she got to the foot of the hill, travelling too fast, and held out her hands to grasp the barbed-wire fence at the bottom. But after all, she was lucky. Leebert, the Virgin Valley headman, was standing in the road looking towards the rolling hills of the farm. He was a wiry man of about fifty, and one look at Annabell told him what was wrong.

"Where de fire is?" he asked, holding her arm to steady her. "Jus' catch you breat' an' tell me. Is de 'ouse?"

She shook her head, her chest heaving painfully.

"Alright. Is mus' de cane-piece, den. Let me call Charlie an' some a de bwoy-dem. Is de cane-piece 'gainst de road-side?"

She nodded as hard as she could. Little black things were swimming before her eyes. Why was Leebert so slow?

"Alright. Ah comin' right now." He turned and faced up the road where a trim blue cottage was set in some distance from the roadside. "Charlie! Mirrie! *Charlie!* Bring me machete an' de two bucket-pan an' come 'ere!"

He made Annabell sit down on the bank at the side of the road. Leebert was at his best in disaster. In a very short time he had set off up the shortcut with Charlie, and his friends Rupert, Alphanso, and Tiny, who had been playing a quiet game of dominoes in the cocoa piece beyond Leebert's house. Even Chicken-foot, his six-year-old nephew, was sent off to call Mr Jones down the road, while Mirrie was told to mix sugar-and-water for Annabell.

Meanwhile Peter and Mr Ferguson were getting two mules harnessed to the smallest cart. They did not speak. There was no time for that. Dennis, Maud, and Mrs Ferguson had assembled all the pails, buckets, and washpans the house afforded, and stood silent and tense as Peter and his father worked. Everything except the fire seemed to move so slowly. Dennis could hear the crackle of the flames growing louder and louder. He wondered if the fire would climb up the hillside to the house, and what would they do if the house caught fire too. There was a set, calm look on his father's face that was more frightening than anything else. He held tightly to his mother's hand and watched. After an age the cart was drawn up in the back yard under the iron water tank that stood there on a high concrete platform. Peter and Dad were rolling out an empty barrel from the tool house. They laid a plank from the back of the cart to the ground, and rolled the barrel up into the cart. It was the only barrel they had. Quickly all of the other containers were put in the cart, and the tedious business of filling them began. Before they were half way through Leebert arrived with his band of fire-fighters. Mrs Ferguson would not let Dennis go with them. Instead he was sent down the short cut to meet Annabell, and make sure that she was all right. Maud compelled Mrs Ferguson to drink a glass of wine and go upstairs and change, while she herself went off to set out a bottle of rum and glasses against the return of the fire-fighting party.

It was a small fire and was put out with far less trouble than is usual with cane-fires. Leebert reckoned that it could not have been burning more than a few minutes when Peter saw it. But in the dry windy weather they would have had no hope at all of stopping it if the alarm had not been raised at once. The cart made three trips back to the tank, but the last two were for damping down the ground where the men cleared a firebreak. Peter's job was to drive the cart along the interval and back to the house, where he and Charlie filled the barrel and washpan from the tank. It was they who brought the good news that the fire was under control, and took Annabell and Dennis down with the second load of water, so that they could help by getting in the way and covering themselves all over in ashes and soot.

That night, after the last well-wisher and assistant had drained the umpteenth tumbler of rum-and-water, Mrs Ferguson brought out a light supper of cocoa, bread, and saltfish fritters on a tray to the verandah. The lamps were lit inside, and sent a warm light through the windows on to the brown, unpolished wood of the verandah. The same north wind that had fanned the fire now played innocently in the tinkling beaded fringes of the gold lampshade.

"Peter," said Mr Ferguson, sitting down in one of the heavy verandah chairs. "Peter, if you hadn't been disobedient today, we would all be in serious trouble now."

He looked steadily at Peter, an odd smile on his face. "In fact you disobeyed twice, didn't you?"

Peter looked down at his feet. Suddenly he felt very tired, and like bursting into tears. Dennis and Annabell paid all their attention to the buttering of bread and the passing of dishes. It was awful.

"Well, didn't you?" repeated Dad, still in that odd, gentle voice.

"Yes, Dad. I should have been in my room, and I shouldn't have gone up to the roof at all." The tears were burning Peter's eyes.

"Quite right," went on their father. "You all know very well what your mother and I think of behaviour of that kind. On the other hand, none of us would have seen the fire at all if we had stayed in our rooms. Not until it was too late. So you see how right and wrong can get mixed up in one another so that it's hard to tell which is which."

Peter nodded. He dared not trust his voice.

"If it were not for the emergency, you would have been severely punished. And I know, only too well, what this night would be like if that fire had gone unchecked. So I cannot punish you. I am too thankful for what you have done in making the alarm in time. So I suppose you must get your reward." Annabell held her breath and Dennis stopped eating. "Don't worry, I said *reward*. If you did do anything wrong, make up for it yourself!" He laughed a clear, ringing laugh. "We're putting in the new pump tomorrow. Your uncle Edwin is coming from Montego Bay tomorrow to supervise the installation. You can stay home from school–" an envious gasp went up from the other two– "and learn something about machinery."

"Oh!" Peter's eyes shone like stars.

"Mind you, just for one or two days. You'll have to do extra work in the evening to keep up, but this is a good chance for you to learn a little mechanical engineering, and Annabell can take a letter to the headteacher excusing you from classes for two days."

Peter, choking on his bread and cocoa, could hardly utter a sound. He managed to say thank you, and was very glad when their mother asked Annabell in a matter-of-fact way if she had packed her school bag yet, and was she supposed to take along the straw mats she had made during the holidays? Nothing was said about the binoculars, which Peter rescued from the floor of the balcony after supper. The children went up to bed very quietly, for once, feeling that the day had been sufficiently exciting in spite of the departure of Uncle Simon Peter. Mr and Mrs Ferguson stayed a long time on the verandah, talking in the dark.

Chapter Four

As soon as they had all finished in the bathroom, Peter, looking a bit ashamed, told Dennis and Annabell that he was sorry about being so mean, and he had something very queer to tell them.

The two boys followed Annabell into her room, where they would not be easily overheard from the front verandah.

"And we've had enough drama and tribulation for one day!" said Annabell, who sometimes liked to use long words.

"It won't take long," said Peter, sitting on the window sill in his pyjamas. Then he paused and seemed reluctant to go on.

"Well, what is it?" asked Annabell impatiently. Dennis was yawning.

"Promise not to laugh?" His voice sounded strange.

"Yes, yes! Promise anything. Just hurry up before Mamma and Dad catch us out of bed! And I'm dying to sleep!" answered Annabell crossly.

"Well, I saw Great Aunt Flossie today, from the

roof. That's when I dropped the binoculars."

"What!" cried Annabell. "Don't believe you! How d'you know who it was, if you really *did* see somebody?"

Dennis sat up on the bed and stared at Peter.

"S-sh! You don't have to bawl at me! Of course I know Great Aunt Flossie! And I saw her real good, because I was using the binoculars, Miss Fool-fool!" He came and sat on the bed beside the other two. "Just listen now: I wanted to try out the binoculars to see if there were any ships over by Montego Bay, and I did see two that were there for a long time. That's why I stayed up there so long, watching them until they started to move again. After that there was nothing else to watch at sea, so I turned the glasses all round the hills up there–" he waved an arm towards Somerton. "It's fun. You can see the houses over there right close up. I even saw a woman washing clothes!"

"Yes, yes," broke in Annabell. "But what about Aunt Flossie? I suppose *she* was washing the clothes!"

"Wait a minute and let me finish," said Peter patiently. "I had just thought I'd better be coming down when I caught sight of a person walking along the interval in the cane-field, down at the bottom of the hill. Not where the fire was. On the other side. I thought, that's queer; who'd be down there now? So I trained the glasses on the person, and saw a tall lady walking down the track away from the house. She had on a big hat, as if she was going to church, and her dress was long, sweeping the grass. I never saw anybody in such a long dress, except at weddings. I was just wondering who on earth she could be, and what did she want in the cane-field all dressed up like that, when she turned around and looked straight up at the house, and straight at me. That's how I know for sure. The

binoculars show you things as clear as day."

The other two waited breathlessly.

"It's so stupid. I clean forgot she's dead, and all I thought was, 'Gosh! She's going to come home any minute now and tell Dad I'm up here!' Next thing I dropped the glasses on the roof and had to grab for them before they slid off entirely. I caught them just in time, and when I looked back, she wasn't there any more. I started to climb down, but what with holding the binoculars and wanting to get another look just to see if there really was somebody in the interval, I made a lot of noise and nearly fell off the roof. I was just taking a last look before climbing over the edge of the roof when I saw the smoke, and there was the fire blazing in the other field. So I jumped."

"You should have told Dad and Mamma," said Annabell, and stopped.

"Why?" asked Dennis.

"They wouldn't believe me," said Peter.

"Tell them all the same," said Annabell, suddenly remembering the laughing voice in the wind on the night before.

"I'm not *scared,* you know," Peter explained scornfully. "I wasn't scared *at all*, any time. At least, only of what Dad would do if he caught me, and later on of the fire. It was going so fast. And anyway they'll say it must have been somebody like Mrs Jones, or Ivy, and I *know* it wasn't. I could see her face, and, and–" his eyes widened suddenly. "Annabell, she was wearing the watch! It was on the chain, round her neck! That's how I knew for sure!"

"But it's right here, in its box!" Annabell leapt out of bed and picked up the little blue box. Sure enough, the silver watch and chain were there, nestling in their bed of cottonwool.

"Well, I don't understand," said Peter, staring at the silver watch. "But they'll just laugh at us, I know that." A note of doubt crept in his voice. "Of course I didn't really get a second look through the glasses. In fact, I didn't get another look at her at all."

"H'mmm," Annabell hugged her knees.

"Well, it doesn't sound like anything much after all," said Peter. "I guess we'd better go to bed now. Come on, Dennis, you can't go to sleep there!"

He dragged Dennis off Annabell's bed and out into the passage, and soon all three of them were fast asleep.

Peter's story did not seem to make much sense to any of the children, after all, and even Peter himself forgot all about it as the days and weeks went by in a perfectly ordinary way, marked only by a thunder-storm in March, school-inspection in April, and the disappointing size and quality of the Easter buns that year. Annabell heard no more strange voices and all of them were more taken up with the new pump, the buggy their father bought, and the prospect of Peter going away to school in Montego Bay, if he managed to win a scholarship that year. Uncle Simon Peter came back for short visits in February and April, but when he returned at the end of May the *Freya* stayed only twenty-four hours in port, and all they had was a letter posted in Montego Bay by Uncle Edwin. The letter warned that his visits would be more uncertain for a while, and there might be changes on the *Freya*, but that was all.

The Fergusons had no radio, but they followed the war news reported in *The Daily Gleaner,* and the children read all about events like the retreat from Dunkirk and the Battle of Britain in a special war magazine brought by Uncle Simon Peter on one of his visits. Dennis had vivid nightmares of the blitz, all mixed up with geography lessons about volcanoes and geysers. Peter and Annabell used to go after school to watch the men drilling on Mr Faulkner's common; they were mostly young fellows of Charlie's age and younger, in tattered clothes and old shoes, if shoes they wore at all. They drilled with sticks instead of rifles, sternly disciplined by World War One veteran Sgt. Moses Mackenzie as they sang

"Solja take de uniform an' go-o-o,
Solja take de uniform an' go!"

The head teacher of the Somerton Government School was appointed A.R.P. warden, and the people of Somerton were told to take refuge in the limestone caves of the area in the event of air-raids. The search for suitable caves became one of the main pursuits of the older boys at school, Peter included. But the biggest event of the year was the film-show held in the schoolroom, where the children saw a war movie entitled *Pastor Hall*. It terrified Dennis, who had never seen a movie before, and even Annabell and Peter could not quite forget the scenes in which the hero, a priest who courageously opposes the Nazis in Germany, is captured, imprisoned, and tortured by the Gestapo. The scenes of grim prison corridors, steel-helmeted and jack-booted guards in black SS uniforms, and on every face the shadows of cruelty and fear haunted their dreams for a long time after. Mrs Ferguson had to leave a lamp burning in the passage at night, for Dennis suddenly grew frightened of the dark, and would not go upstairs at night without Peter or Annabell.

The children had long discussions with school friends, and among themselves at home, on the subject of the war. In the summer holidays Dennis refused to go in the backyard for days because he thought that the water tank was what army tanks are made from, and there could be Germans hiding in it. A boy at school told him that if Hitler won the war, he was going to bring back slavery in Jamaica starting with black people and working up to Chinese and East Indians. " 'Im will take you brother an' sister first t'ing," said his tormentor matter-of-factly, "an' all like you will 'ave to clean 'im shoes an' carry 'im top-hat an' cane while *dem* chain up in de cellar under de 'ouse like dog. You lucky you so white. 'Im 'ave puss-eye same like you." Mrs Ferguson found him staining himself with dark brown Kiwi shoe-polish, and gave him a spanking. It was Annabell who cheered him up, creeping into his room with half a bullah as a gift, and the news that Peter had threatened to fight any boy he heard telling Dennis rubbish like that.

"But- but- Annabell, d'you think it's true? Really true?" The bullah was disappearing fast, despite his many woes.

Annabell sat cross-legged on the floor. She looked at the stains of polish on Dennis's hands and face, and tried not to laugh.

"I don't know. Dad says it's just people talking, he doesn't think anybody knows. Ask Dad or Mamma. I don't know." She would not say any more, for in truth she was just as frightened as Dennis, but would not have shown it for the world. She thought about the war far more than either of her brothers, but it frightened her too much to let her talk about it to anyone, even to her mother. That was why she hated Peter's pictures of aeroplanes and tanks. Every one of them was real to Annabell, and though she did not wake up scared in the night like Dennis, she had two dreams that came back over and over again until she knew them by heart. One was of a bright moonlight night at Virgin Valley, with all of them waiting in the house for some unknown but dreaded event. The doors and windows were all open, waiting; there was not a sound anywhere. And then the cane-fields rippled, once, twice, and long lines of armed men (friend or foe, she never knew), stole up the hill past the house and into the forest behind. The other dream was more violent, but somehow not as chilling as those silent battalions. In the second dream she was at school, sitting in Fourth Class with all the other children. Suddenly a horn blew, and the next instant great black planes roared over the high hills from the north and rained bombs on the school. She went on sitting up straight at her desk between Lillian Chin and Phyllis Griffiths, as fountains of earth and fire leaped up in the schoolyard, while Miss Richards tapped on her desk and said in a sharp little voice, "Now children, Jamaica is a tropical island north of the Equator."

She wished she dared ask Uncle Simon Peter what it was like at sea, in war-time. But he never stayed long, and they were not supposed to ask him things like that. Most of the children at school were afraid of the Germans, and even the thought of seeing a real live German, unarmed and alone, made Annabell cold with fright. None of her friends thought of Germans as ordinary people, and were very surprised and unbelieving when Miss Richards showed the class pictures of German women and children working peacefully in a farm yard. Her best friend Lillian looked under her bed every single night to make sure there wasn't a German hiding under there. Annabell did not think that Germans could get into Virgin Valley without a lot of people knowing first, so she did not search under her bed, or in the closet, at bed time. But she hoped that Uncle Simon Peter did look under his bed, or rather in his bunk on the *Freya*, for there was no telling what might happen at sea.

One of Uncle Simon Peter's first gifts long ago had been a globe for Peter, when he first started out at school. It was not a very big globe, like those used in class, but quite big enough for you to read such names as Berlin, Moscow, London, Amsterdam, Aden and Singapore. It even had Kingston and Montego Bay marked, very, very small. Mr Ferguson and Peter kept coloured pins stuck here and there to show where the fighting was going on: and there was a special row of pins across the Atlantic, where the German submarines roamed. Of all things, the three children felt that to be torpedoed at sea was worst of all. None of them could swim, and they knew anyway that swimming is not much use when you are hundreds of miles from land.

"The sea is very cold," said Peter when they discussed it. "You have to get into the lifeboats."

"Suppose you haven't got any?" asked Dennis.

"Every ship has life-boats, stupid, and life-jackets too! I thought you knew that!" exclaimed Annabell. "But those can't go far, you know. You can't cross the Atlantic in a life-boat. It's much too small! It's handy only when you're shipwrecked on the coast, or another ship comes by and picks you up. If you sank in the middle of the sea, a life-boat wouldn't be much good at all. It would take months to reach land, like Columbus coming over here! You'd starve long before you got to land!"

Peter started to dispute this point, and then was not sure but that she might be right after all.

"Uncle Simon Peter can swim," said Dennis

stubbornly. "He taught Uncle Edwin to swim. He could get away that way, couldn't he? Couldn't he keep swimming until another ship found him? Somebody would go and search for him, because he sends out *beacons*. He told me so himself last time he was here. All he has to do is send out a beacon, and a ship will come and pick him up same time!"

Peter and Annabell gave up trying to explain to him. He always ended every argument with a statement that nothing could ever happen to Uncle Simon Peter; they knew better. Peter took comfort in thinking about the supposed strength of the British navy, and Uncle Simon Peter's skill as a sailor. After all, he had been in the last war too, though not for much of it. Annabell tried not to think about it at all.

But in spite of their worries, Uncle Simon Peter seemed to be carrying on as well as ever. He came back in June, just before Peter's examinations, and spent three whole days. There were no presents for the children, but they knew better than to whine for presents at a time like that, when thousands of people were suffering starvation and worse. Uncle Simon Peter promised to teach them all to swim, and told Dennis that he was not afraid of Germans, well, not very much, and laughed when Mrs Ferguson begged him to stay in Jamaica and let someone else take over the *Freya*. After he left, they started to have family prayers every night, after supper, instead of just on Sundays, and they always ended by singing one verse of 'Eternal Father, strong to save.' Even though they sang it every night, Annabell could not bear to sing the words "For those in peril on the sea." She could only move her lips and let the others do the singing.

Dennis's birthday fell in July, in the middle of the

summer holidays, and all three children hoped that Uncle Simon Peter would be back for that. But a letter came saying that the *Freya* would not be coming to Jamaica for a while, with a long black patch in the centre of the page where the censor had struck out something. Mrs Ferguson looked very worried, and Maud shook her head over it, but Mr Ferguson said that perhaps the *Freya* had been assigned some less dangerous task. Nobody believed that, not even the children, but no more was said on the subject.

Then one day in September an official-looking letter arrived, announcing that Peter had won a place as a day pupil at Cornwall College, and would be taken into the school in the January term of the following year. It was very exciting, and everyone was proud of him, but it meant that for the first time the three children would not be together any more. Peter pleaded in vain to be allowed to take the Adelphi bus daily to Montego Bay. Their parents were firm. It was too far to walk to the bus-line, and petrol rationing might soon make the bus-service even more erratic than it already was. He would have to go and live in Montego Bay, and board with an old spinster school-teacher who had been a friend of Aunt Flossie's, and walk to school daily. He would not have minded living with Uncle Edwin, but Uncle Edwin was a bachelor working round the clock at Barnet sugar factory, and he had nowhere to put up a schoolboy, even if Mrs Ferguson had considered him old and dull enough to have charge of her eldest child.

Chapter Five

It was a grey and drizzly afternoon in November when Annabell was helping her mother with the tedious task of making Peter's new uniforms, that the familiar sound of the Austin engine was heard on the drive. Annabell and her mother both looked up at the same time. They sprang up from the dining table where Mrs Ferguson had been cutting and basting khaki shirts, letting a pile of half-done work fall to the floor. Annabell threw away the shirt and box of buttons she was holding and darted through the door before her mother could utter a word.

Sure enough, there was the little car struggling up the driveway, and the white-haired figure towering over the steering wheel.

"Uncle Simon Peter!" gasped Annabell, as the car shuddered to a stop in front of the house. The blue eyes shone mischievously at her as the door opened and she was lost in the great bear-like hug that smelt as always of rich tobacco, bayrum, and Yardley's shaving soap.

"Peggy and my little Anna!" They were both swept into another vast embrace as Uncle Simon Peter reached the shallow steps of the verandah. "You look well, very well! Where are Yoe and the boys? And my good Maud?"

"How white his hair is!" thought Annabell. But the hand on her shoulder grasped her with as much strength and firmness as ever.

At a word from her mother, Annabell ran off to fetch

her father and brothers, and to shout to Maud, ironing in her room, that the Captain was here and calling for her.

The dining table was hastily cleared, Maud's ironing put aside, and everyone bustled around helping as best they could. The children got under everyone's feet, but no one minded. The lamps were lit, and a bottle of pimento dram set out on a tray with tiny gold-rimmed glasses for the grown-ups. Annabell and Dennis crept into the nook of Uncle Simon Peter's chair, where they hoped to remain unnoticed and exempt from errands and chores.

They asked all sorts of questions about the *Freya*, the air-raids in London, and if Uncle Simon Peter had seen any submarines, but he only shook his head and laughed. Then Mr Ferguson told them not to plague him, and the talk turned to local news, and especially to news of the farm and the Ferguson family. Uncle Simon Peter was pleased to hear of Peter's scholarship, and then all of the children were made to stand against his back, one after the other, to show how much they had grown in the last five months.

"How long will you stay this time, Uncle Simon Peter?" Dennis alone had the courage to ask the question that was in everybody's minds.

The old man pulled Dennis's ears gently.

"Tomorrow morning I must go," he said "Perhaps next time I can stay longer."

Then he turned to Peter and wanted to know how they were getting on with the binoculars, and whether they had seen any of the warships that visited Jamaica. Later on, after supper, he went out to the car and came back with his hands behind his back, grinning broadly.

"Well, all we ever talk about is war, war, war!

Everybody, even Dennis, thinks of yust war and war and war! I make something for you while on my last trip, so we don't think of only war forever, eh? Your Great Aunt would not agree that we always think of what is wicked and ugly. So I finish this for you, which I started for her long ago, and put aside for the last six years."

He brought his right hand from behind his back and held out a model ship on the palm of his great hand. It was about ten inches long, no more, and a perfect replica of the *Freya*. This time the children were too stunned to say anything at all. While Uncle Simon Peter was explaining that this was modelled on the peace-time *Freya*, and painted in her proper colours, the three children took the little ship from him and saw that it was a marvellous, faultless copy of the steamship, complete with pennants, smokestack, life-boats, everything.

"What's this, Uncle Simon Peter?" Dennis was turning the model ship around in his hands, and now he pointed to a queer little carving on the underside of the tiny ship. It was a boar's head, cut deep into the wood of the prow. "Why did you put that there?"

"That's just like the links on Aunt Flossie's chain!" cried Annabell, peering at the little carved face. It was very small, no wider than a sixpence was in those days.

"Oh well, yust for good luck, that is there," Uncle Simon Peter smiled. "All sailors believe in luck, you know. That is an old sign for good luck in Norway. Many of the Nielsens had that sign on their boats, some where or other. Why, my cousin Gustav, who was – how is it in English? – oh, yes, a landlubber he was, only using a dinghy to fish from, in summer; even *he* carved it on the prow of his boat, and him a dockside sailor!"

They all laughed at that, but Uncle Simon Peter knew nothing of the meaning of the charm, and could not say what sort of luck it was supposed to bring. The talk passed on to other matters, and the boar's head was forgotten. The children took the little ship up to bed with them, and debated where it should be kept. They felt that this was even more important a gift than the binoculars, compass, and watch, and so they tried to share it fairly among themselves as their uncle would have liked. But it is not easy for three to share one small model ship, even in the same house, and when Peter left for school in January, what would they do then?

At last Peter made the only suggestion that would work, though it cost him a lot to do so.

"You know, I think the ship must stay here, with the other things, I mean. It sort of belongs with them. And I don't expect that old Miss French will let me keep things like this at the boarding house. It might get broken, or the other boys there might interfere with it. Let's keep it one at a time, each of us in turn, and you two will have it when I'm in Montego Bay."

He looked so miserable that Annabell began to beg him to take it with him, and started to suggest possible hiding places in his trunk or schoolbag, but he was firm. At last they agreed to do as he said, but Annabell insisted that he should have the first and longest turn, since he would have to do without it all of the next term.

"And Dad says you'll be coming home some weekends, so *of course* you''ll have it then!" cried Annabell.

This cheered him up considerably. He had almost been on the point of deciding not to go to Cornwall College after all. And it did help, in the long days when no more news came of the *Freya* or her captain, to look at that solid little ship with the boar's head staring impudently from the prow. Christmas came and went very quietly, with a smaller Christmas tree than usual, fewer presents, and rain on Boxing Day. Uncle Edwin came to spend the Christmas holiday, bringing some precious fireworks for the children with which they terrified the dogs and got themselves in trouble with Maud and their mother. Uncle Edwin, grinning, was told off properly by Maud.

"You don' know you a big man now? Look pan de stove what me clean yesiday! All de h'ashes blow pan de floor an' dutty de place! Fram me born me never see big man gwaan like pickney so much! Saviour give me patience!" And she seized a broom and drove them from the kitchen. Her last words followed them across the back yard. "Is dat mek no woman want fi married to you! Tek clappers an' throw in de fireplace like pickney; ef Captain did de ya, unnu woulda behave unnu self an' don' come trouble poor ol' lady kitchen!"

The 'poor ol' lady' was Maud herself, of course, who did not care tuppence for squibs, rockets, or thunderbolts, but was mad because someone had dared to invade her sanctuary. She always treated Uncle Edwin much as she treated the three children, partly because he was so much younger than Mr Ferguson, and mostly because he had been the baby at Barnet Street, and she could not really think of him as anything else.

But that night Maud had one of her dreams. These did not come very often, and none of the other grownups seemed to take them seriously. At breakfast time Annabell was sent out to the kitchen to ask for another jug of coffee and more fried dumplings for Uncle Edwin. She stopped dead in the doorway at the sight which met her eyes. Maud was sitting on the floor in front of the stove, her shoulders bowed, her hands clasped tightly over her bosom, and on her head a white cloth sprinkled with ashes and cinders from the fire. She must have just done that, for the cloth was actually smoking still in some spots, and there was ash on the floor all around the stove, in fact far more than Uncle Edwin's squib had scattered the day before.

"Maud, please," began Annabell in a small voice, wondering whether she ought to address her at all, and wanting to run back to the safety of the dining room.

"Fall on your knees an' pray, chile! Pray for de sinners who mek de wrongs an' walk with Satan! Pray for de innocent! An' pray for de Captain in de bowels of de whale, may he cast up on dry land, God preserve us!"

Annabell felt she ought to do something, but while she wanted to show Maud that she did understand, partly, she did not want to kneel on the kitchen floor, which was cold and very hard. Also, there was the matter of the coffee. Luckily for her, her father's voice could be heard at the back door saying that they should be getting ready to leave for town, and not be sitting over the breakfast table until all hours. At that Maud beckoned to Annabell to help her rise, clutched at her shoulder with a claw of a hand, and took the coffee pot from her.

In a short while the children's parents had left with Uncle Edwin, Mrs Ferguson to take her Red Cross fund collection to the office in Montego Bay, and to buy new school books for Annabell and Dennis, and Mr Ferguson to see the solicitor in St. James Street who handled the affairs of the farm. Mrs Ferguson also wanted to take a present for Miss French, and so have an opportunity to make a surreptitious inspection of that stern lady's domain, a fact of which Miss French was quite aware. Beyond telling the children to behave well while they were out, and to expect them home quite late, perhaps after bed-time, Mrs Ferguson gave no more thought to anything at Virgin Valley. Mr Ferguson handed her into the front seat of the Barnet Estate van, which Uncle Edwin was able to borrow from time to time, and they all set off for Montego Bay.

It was a beautiful, clear morning after the rain of the previous day, and of course Peter was up on the roof with the binoculars in time to see the van turn the corner of the main road where they went on their walks. Annabell and Dennis were inside, Annabell making her bed and grumbling, and Dennis cleaning his shoes so as to have no jobs to remember and be bothered about for the rest of the day. He did not clean them very well, for the sunlight was making a brilliant patch on the bathroom floor in front of him, and he could hear Peter on the roof above. He and Annabell had almost finished their tasks when they heard Maud coming upstairs. She had flung the ash-streaked cloth over her head again, and she was out of breath from the stairs, but she no longer looked wild and grief-stricken.

"Call you brother," she said to Dennis. "Me 'ave someting to say to de t'ree a you."

There was something about her that made Dennis obey at once. Peter was none too pleased at having to come down again, but Maud's summons could not be lightly disregarded. She did not tell on one, and she did not spank, but at times there was a look in her eye that made the bravest quail; for weeks after, the offender would meet no welcome in the kitchen, and Mamma always guessed what had happened without being told anything about it.

As soon as Peter entered, Maud sat on the chair by Annabell's bed and looked at them.

"A message" (she pronounced it 'metches') "come for de t'ree of you."

Dennis looked surprised, but Annabell and Peter waited.

"Missis come to me las' night, an' tell me certain t'ings." Her glasses began to mist over, and she paused a while. Then she went on in a strong voice. "She appear beside me in de night, in 'ar weddin' dress what she married to Captain in, but she did 'ave a bunch of red, red roses in 'ar 'ands, red like blood. She was cryin' an' cryin', an' she say to me, 'Maud, Maud, I can' let go de flowers to wipe my eye, call Captain to wipe dem for me.' So me say, 'But Missis, Captain no de ya; Captain gaan to sea.' So she cry more, an' say 'Why 'im gaan, an' now 'im is ole an' tired?' So me say to 'ar, 'But Missis, don't you know is war goin' on, an' Captain gaan to sea?' Den she 'old up 'ar 'ead straight, an' me see dat wid all she was cryin', she look good, an' 'andsome, jus' like when she an' Captain get marry. But de water was runnin' from 'ar two eye like river. Den she say to me, 'Why nobody never tell me? Why unnu never tell me, eeeeh? An' nobody to wipe me eye for me, nobody but de children-dem, an' dem so small.' So me believe is you Daddy an' you Uncle h'Edwin she talkin', for she dead over six year now, an' all a unnu was small-small baby dat time. But before me could answer, she come right up to de bedside an' say to me, 'Tell de t'ree little children to 'elp we, me an' Captain. Give dem de metches, an' pray for de worl'. Don' forget fi tell dem: Peter, h'Annabell, an' Dennis, an' pray for de sins of de worl'.' An' same time me find meself sittin' up in bed, an' day light outside."

She sighed deeply and looked at them one by one.

Annabell felt frightened, and Peter was shuffling to his feet.

"What are we supposed to do?" asked Dennis, who was very confused by the whole affair. "Why must we do something?"

"Me don't know. You mus' find dat out unnu self." Maud got up and pulled the cloth off her head, suddenly brisk and business-like. "Me 'ave me work fi finish. Me can' stay up 'ere an' waste time like pickney."

With that she went off to dust the drawing room, and no more was to be had out of her on the subject.

"What was all that for?" asked Dennis again. The three children were once more on the roof with the binoculars. The day was still bright, but a cold north wind promised clouds and even rain by noon. The wind kept turning over the backs of the leaves in flurries so that the neighbouring hills were stippled with a silver-grey sheen instead of their usual deep, bluish-green.

"It's only a dream after all," said Peter, as though he was actually thinking something quite different, but preferred not to say what it was.

"It's *queer*, though." Annabell sat astride the crown of the roof enjoying the heat of the sun on her back and the coldness of the wind in her face. "I wonder if something is happening to Uncle Simon Peter? But I don't see why the three of us should be in the dream. I can *hardly* remember Aunt Flossie, and Dennis doesn't really know her at all!"

"Maud drank two long glasses of rum and sorrel in the kitchen last night," reported Dennis. "Uncle Edwin gave her."

Annabell giggled.

"Last Good Friday she dreamed that the spring flooded and washed away the house. Remember? And she wanted Dad to move all of us out of the house, but not a thing happened," said Peter.

"Oh yes! That was when we were having the drought!" added Annabell. "Maud's dreams are very queer. But all the same, I don't like them. And I don't like this one at all, at all!"

That summed it up for the three children. Annabell shivered slightly as the words 'Tell de t'ree children to 'elp we, me an' Captain' came unbidden to her mind later in the day. The boys appeared to have dismissed it all as too peculiar for them to make head or tail of, and better forgotten.

The day turned out to be very good fun after all. They spent most of the morning on the roof, and saw four ships go by. When the sky went cloudy, they came down and played eight games of dominoes, of which Peter won four, and Annabell and Dennis two each. Then they helped Charlie start the water pump, and came back dirty and happy for a late lunch of stewed gungo peas and run-down, accompanied by roast plantain and yam, and washed down with orange juice. In the afternoon they went with Fred and Lillian Chin in search of a cave on the hill where the spring rises, with the intention of establishing an air-raid shelter up there for themselves. By evening they were filthy from head to foot, tired out, and very happy. Dennis and Annabell shook hands on the fulfilment of their vow, made at breakfast that morning, not to wash or tidy *at all* for the whole, live-long day. Maud was in a benign mood, and let them have their supper with her in the kitchen, instead of at the dining table with its starched cloth, its table napkins in rings, and the air of sitting up straight and minding your manners which hung over it even in their parents' absence. Peter and Dennis sat on the warm doorstep sipping their mugs of cocoa, while Maud sat in the armchair by the kitchen table with Annabell on a stool in front of the stove.

All of a sudden, Annabell found herself saying, "Maud, what does Aunt Flossie want us to do?"

The two boys looked up.

Maud took off her glasses and wiped them on the hem of her apron.

"Don't me tell you say me no know?" she sounded peevish. "What you h'askin' me for? 'Ow me mus' know? Don't is yourself to know? Don't h'ask me not'ing about it; me don't responsible. But one t'ing me can tell you: my Missis is a Christian woman, a strong woman. Don't forget dat."

She suddenly became sulky and cross, and began taking note of the state of their clothes. They thought it wise to get out of the way, and went up to wash for bed after leaving a lamp turned down on the drawing room table for their parents, and another on the landing where Dennis could see its glow.

Chapter Six

Annabell felt lonely and nervous after she had said good night to the boys and climbed into bed. The sheets were damp and chilly, and her feet refused to get warm. She lay stiff and motionless in the middle of the bed, feeling colder and colder, and getting wider awake as she grew colder. The wind was blowing through the window above the landing, causing the light of the lamp to dance in unsteady waves across the pale, white-washed walls of her room. She wondered how Dennis could stand it. Her hands were very cold; a draught crept down the back of her neck and made her teeth chatter. She wondered if she should go and get in bed with the boys, but Peter was a bad sleeper who kicked, rolled, and threw the bedclothes on the floor. Then she remembered the heavy cardigan which her mother had knitted for herself, and then had found that it was just a trifle too small. It was much too big for Annabell, and it was pink, a colour she loathed, but Mamma had said it would be useful some day, and with wool being so scarce and so dear Annabell might count herself lucky. She slid out of bed and tugged at the bottom drawer of the bureau in the corner of the room. There was the cardigan lying wrapped in tissue paper at the back of the drawer. As she pulled it out something fell out and hit lightly against her bare feet. She started, then realised that it wasn't a mouse or anything horrible. She peered at it in the half-dark and saw, to her surprise, that it was the little cardboard and leather box in which Aunt Flossie's watch and chain were kept. That's funny, she thought, picking up the heavy little box, who could have put it in the bottom drawer under the sweater? It's supposed to be in the small top drawer, with the clean handkerchiefs and ribbons. But for some reason she did not put it back in the bureau, though she could easily have done so. Instead she pulled on the thick cardigan, and climbed back into bed with the box clutched tightly in her hand under the pillow

In the middle of the night Annabell woke up. She had been having a very pleasant dream, which she kept trying to prolong as she drifted up into consciousness. The dream had something to do with flying over a marvellous bazaar full of the most gorgeous toys and strange, colourful ornaments: robes of yellow silk, blue, green and fire-red satins gleaming between bunches of feathers and coloured beads that were lit by hanging lamps each carved out of single, enormous, precious stone. She was flying along simply by holding her arms out straight and jumping into the air. Peter and Dennis were there too, but the dream stopped just as she was flying through the lane of the sweet-makers, where there was the most mouth-watering display of chocolates, toffee, and fudge. She woke up to find the box still in her hand, and her fingers gone to sleep.

'So *that's* what woke me up!' she thought crossly, pulling her hand from under the pillow and starting to reach out to the bedside table. The lamp in the passage was still flickering dimly. Her fingers opened stiffly to set the box on the table when she heard the sound of the piano downstairs played very quietly. 'Mamma and Dad must have come back at last!' she thought sleepily. 'I wonder why Mamma's playing the piano now?'' Her fingers curled around the box again, and she began to listen to the clear, remote melody floating from the drawing room at the other end of the house. It was a pretty song; she knew some of the words herself. Tomorrow she must ask Mamma to teach her all of it. She would copy out the words in her song book, where she had the verses of her favourite songs, 'Slide, Mongoose', 'Old Black Joe', and 'Don't Fence Me In'. She forgot about her stiff fingers and the dream, and followed the thin, bright tune of the song:

Blow the wind southerly, southerly, southerly,
Blow the wind south o'er the bonnie blue sea,
Blow the wind southerly, southerly, southerly,
Blow, bonnie breeze, my true love to me.

The thought of Uncle Simon Peter and Aunt Flossie

came to her briefly, vividly, as she fell deeper into sleep, clasping the box tightly to her in both hands.

The next thing she knew, it was morning and sunlight was flooding the room with bright gold. She had overslept. The boys's voices rang out from the front verandah, and she could hear Maud scolding the two dogs by the back door. Her mother was calling up the stairs.

"Annabell! Annabell! What's keeping you, child?"

She jumped out of bed and washed and dressed in a hurry. Much later, when she was making her bed, she found the little box under the pillow. As she picked it up, she remembered the song and her last strange thought about Uncle Simon Peter. She was busy getting ready for the special children's service of carols and lessons, which was being held at eleven o'clock that day, but she dashed out of her room with the back of her dress half done up, and called to her mother who was putting on her hat in front of the wardrobe mirror.

"Mamma, could you give me the words of that song you were playing for Dad last night?" she asked breathlessly, fumbling with the sash of her pale green organdy dress.

"Last night? What are you talking about, Annabell?" her glance fell on Annabell and she turned her around and tied the sash to her satisfaction. "What song is this?"

"The song you were playing on the piano last night, Mamma. It's called something like 'Blow the wind southerly' or 'Blow the south wind.' Could I copy the words into my book, please?"

Mrs Ferguson straightened up and looked hard at Annabell.

"Castor oil," she said, very firmly. "I don't know

what's got into you children, and even Maud too. Of course I wasn't playing the piano last night! Your father and I were far too tired when we got home, and it was much too late to think of doing a thing like that. Besides, the piano needs tuning. It's all this rich food you've been having. Peter and Dennis had nightmares too last night, and from what I hear Maud has been doing the same! A good dose of Epsom salts or castor oil is what you all need. Playing the piano indeed!"

But she did find the song for Annabell that evening. It was in a pile of sheet music in the cabinet by the piano where Mrs Ferguson kept her most precious music books, magazines, and embroidery patterns. The yellowing folder of folk songs was beginning to crack at the edges, but it fell open at the right page as if it had been much used. When Annabell turned to the front page to read the list of titles in the hope of finding other treasures, her glance was caught by an inscription:

> "To Florence Annabell Russell, in memory of May 12, 1919, from Yr. Good and Respectful friend, Pieter Nielsen."

The next day was a Monday, and the three children had a long talk about Uncle Simon Peter and Aunt Flossie. They also kept a sharp look-out for the Austin, as everyone felt that it was time for the *Freya* to be back in the Caribbean. New Year's Day was due to fall on the following Thursday, and it would be too much if both Christmas and New Year went by without Uncle Simon Peter. Annabell told the boys about how she had heard the piano playing during the night; while they had heard nothing of the sort, they both had an assortment of nightmares to relate, and they all hoped that by eating their vegetables without a murmur for the next two or three days, the awful threat of castor oil might be averted. In the meanwhile a new set of Chinese checkers was there to be tried out, as well as a jig-saw puzzle of Ali Baba and the forty thieves. But they were all restless, and no one could settle down to anything for long. Annabell was especially distressed, as she felt it was her fault that they might all be dosed that very night.

"I told you that Mamma and Dad won't believe if we tell them about seeing or hearing things." said Peter.

"But they've never said that ghosts don't happen!" protested Annabell. "All Dad says is that *he's* never seen one, and he doesn't know anybody who has."

"Well, what about Uncle Edwin? *He's* seen things!" said Dennis suddenly. They were playing dominoes in a quiet corner of the verandah, and the other two were waiting for him to make his move.

"What d'you mean?" asked Annabell. "Peter, it's your turn after Dennis! Wake up and play, for goodness' sake!" She gave him a sharp nudge.

"Uncle Edwin saw something once when he was little," Dennis continued. "but Dad says it can't really be true 'because your uncle loves to tell good stories, children,' " he dropped his voice in an excellent imitation of their father starting on a lecture. The others giggled.

"Oh *that* story!" Peter made a careful move which effectively blocked the other two players. Amid their groans he continued. "You mean the story about Uncle Edwin on the night before the earthquake? But he was only two or three! He was just learning to talk; that's why Dad says it's all nonsense."

"But what did Uncle Edwin do?" Annabell was suddenly alert. "I want to know *exactly* what happened.

Do *you* know, Peter?"

"You'd better ask Maud. But I don't see how that's going to help at all. And he doesn't even remember anything about it himself. It's Aunt Flossie who told me about it–" he broke off and stared at the other two. "Why, I never thought of that before!"

He sat up, a look of strange concentration on his face, Annabell and Dennis looked up from the game in surprise. He got to his feet and walked slowly over to the verandah railing, staring at the greygreen fields below with a blank expression in his eyes.

"What's biting you?" asked Dennis. "It's your turn again, but you've won anyway. What's got into you?"

"S-sh. I'm thinking." said Peter crossly. Dennis rolled his eyes and tapped his head meaningfully. Annabell looked impatiently at them both, and announced that she was tired of dominoes; she was going to go and ask Maud about Uncle Edwin. She was sure it might be useful. She ran off before Peter could stop her.

Maud was in the kitchen corning beef which had arrived early that morning as a 'New Year's' extra from the Somerton butcher. The kitchen table was strewn with onions, skellions, cloves of garlic, thyme, country peppers, and various other spices. The large yabba was on the floor near her, for it was too heavy for Maud to lift even when it was empty. She was measuring out two cups of salt into a large jug when Annabell raced in.

"One cup, two cup. Lawks! Pickney, where you t'ink you is? Race-track, missis? Ef you lick me down me can' get up, so tek time, missis, tek time, me beg you! Ole lady bone well dry an' easy fi bruck!" But she did not drive Annabell out of the kitchen, or forbid her to approach the table. "Pass me de saltpetre, chile. One teaspoon. Pass a nex' clean teaspoon from de dresser. Look into de drawer. An' don' give me no rusty one."

Annabell passed spoons, washed knives, chopped skellion and garlic, and waited. The mysteries of corning and pickling were explained to her, and the relative merits of corned beef and corned pork described. At last she had her reward. The yabba, covered tightly with a cloth, was dragged into the bottom of the kitchen safe, where it would be secure from the dogs, but cool enough to keep fresh while the salt and spices did their work. Annabell did the dragging, so that Maud would not have to bend her old joints. As she dusted off her hands and knees, she looked up at Maud and asked,

"Maud, please, what was it that Uncle Edwin saw on the night of the 1907 earthquake?"

Maud surveyed her over her glasses. She seemed amused at some private joke.

"You h'uncle h'Edwin? Dat fool-fool bway, call 'imself h'engineer?" she chuckled, wiping her hands on her apron. "Come sweep off 'ere for me!"

Annabell fetched the broom from behind the door, and began sweeping slowly, one eye on Maud. She knew that she would not have to wait long. Maud called to her a few times saying that she wasn't sweeping carefully, then made her gather up all of the rubbish and put it in the garbage pan by the door. At last she was satisfied.

"Well, me ironin' sit down all dis while doin' nottn', Saviour know is only two hand me got." She rose from the armchair breathing hard to show how worn-out and tired she was. Then she winked at Annabell.

"Come sit down inside wid me, Miss Anna, an' sprinkle de t'ings one-one for me."

Annabell ran to fill the big white enamel mug with water. She had won.

"Well, all right now," said Maud, testing one of the flat irons from the coalpot by the doorway. "Me did tell you 'bout dat eart'quake already, but you pickney forget every t'ing quick as lightnin'."

Annabell let her breath out silently. She did not dare even to look at Maud in case she should change her mind. She damped her father's handkerchiefs and collars, after Maud's instructions, and made a separate bundle of the table linen and face-towels. All of the embroidered things had to go together, for they were ironed twice, right side and wrong side through a doubled length of old linen kept for that purpose by Maud herself. Laundry was sacred in Maud's eyes, and any deviation from the ritual on Annabell's part was likely to lead to scolding or angry silence.

"Well, mek me see now." Maud tested another iron and found it satisfactory. "Dat time, you understan', you Gramma an' Grampa was livin' in Kingston, an' you Daddy was a big enough boy, eleven or twelve, I don' remember which. De Edwin-im was a little pickney, just learn to walk an' talk, mus' be two or t'ree years old, because you Gramma did 'ave two more between dem, what never live. Is 'ow dis iron get cold so quick? Put little more coal in de fire for me, chile. Is God mercy mek you Daddy an' you h'uncle come to spend time in Montego Bay when 'im strike Kingston wid h'eart'quake an' fire, or dem woulda dead same like you Gramma, you Grampa, an' Missis first 'usband, Mass Josiah. Well, dat is 'ow life stay, pickney, two are grindin' at de mill: one is taken, de other left. Dem did come down fi New Year 'oliday, an' little time after, you Gramma start to feel sick, so dem decide fi tek 'ar to doctor in Kingston, an' you Grampa an' Mass Joe carry 'ar. You Grampa did want Mass Joe 'elp 'im wid some business, being as de two of dem was carpenter an' builder, an' use to work wid one another before you Grampa move to Kingston. Anyway, dem leave de week before de eart'quake, an' Missis even get a letter say dem reach safe, an' you Gramma feelin' little better."

Annabell had heard all of this many times before. She knew that her grandparents had lived in an old wooden house on Charles Street in Kingston. The spot where the house had stood had been pointed out to them by Dad, when they went to Kingston on a visit in 1939. Dad said that all of the other houses around it had been of the same style, and much the same age. The dry, weathered wood of verandahs, floors, jalousies and shingled roofs had burned like paper. And she knew too that Aunt Flossie had gone to Kingston to search for them, right after the earthquake, leaving Maud in charge of Dad and Uncle Edwin at Barnet Street.

"Well, dem perish in de fire, chile, an' not'ing leave behind to show where dem did live, not'ing at all. Missis never leave Kingston until she search an' search, an' see dat dem was gone forever, Saviour will be done. She say to me, 'Maud, ef is only dem finger leave, me mus' find it.' When Missis mek up 'ar mind fi do anyt'ing, h'angels can do no better. An' she did know from before what comin' to pass."

She stopped ironing and looked at Annabell over her spectacles.

"You Daddy don' like to talk of it to dis day. You musn' blame 'im, for is 'im an' Missis feel de loss, an' 'im lose father an' mother. You h'uncle too small to feel it like 'im. Well, de night before de h'eart'quake, de four of we was upstairs, jus' when it comin' on to night. All of a sudden you h'uncle start to laugh an' point 'im finger out t'rough de door. 'Papa! Papa!' 'im call out, an' me an' you Daddy believe you Grampa mus' be outside, an'we run an' look up an' down, but we don' see anybody at all. So we sit down, an' you h'uncle call out again, "Mamma! Mamma! Papa! Papa!' an' 'im run to de railing an' wave, like 'im wavin' to somebody in de street. So Missis jump up an' she say, 'What wrong wid you, Eddie? Mamma an' Papa in Kingston, dem gone wid Uncle Joe. Dem not 'ere now.' All dis time de little pickney laughin' an' lookin' out, an' she lift 'im up to carry 'im back inside. As she lift 'im up, 'im start to fight an' cry, an' 'im bawl out, 'Mek me see Mamma an' Papa! Dem soon leave, an' dem not comin' back!' 'Im fight so hard she had was to let 'im go, an' 'im run back to de railing before you Daddy or me coulda catch 'im, an' 'im lean 'im 'ead t'rough de railing, an' call out, 'Ta-taa Papa! Ta-taa Mamma!' An' 'im wave 'im 'and."

Maud scraped her throat lengthily.

"Well, after dat 'im come inside quite normal, an' 'ave supper, an' play wid you Daddy. When time come to go to bed, you Auntie carry 'im inside an' 'im say to 'ar, 'Auntie, you love me?' So she say, 'Yes, Eddie, all a we love you. Don't you know dat?' An' 'im look pan 'ar good, a little boy like dat, an' 'im say, 'Mamma tell me to h'ask you, an' Papa say to tell you de 'ouse burn down, an' 'im sorry. Papa say everyt'ing burn up, an' dem not comin' back.' "

There was a long silence. Annabell listened to the spitting of the little coal fire as Maud stirred up the ashes and put in fresh coal. Sparks flew out with a cheerful crack-crack. Annabell dragged her fascinated gaze away from the red-gold caverns of fire.

"Did Aunt Flossie believe him, Maud?" she asked at length. "What did she do when he said all that?"

"What she was to do, Miss Anna?" Maud laid the pile of stiff white collars in the clothes tray beside her. "She come out to me, an' tell me she feel somet'ing is wrong, she feel it in 'ar 'eart, an' she know she not goin' to see Mass Joe, or 'ar brother an' 'im wife again. She h'ask me to pray wid 'ar for all of dem, dat God 'ave mercy on dem, whatever trouble comin' to dem. She bring out 'ar Bible, an' she read Psalm One 'Undred an' T'irty-nine, which was Miss Flossie favourite Bible-readin': Whither shall I go from thy spirit, an' whither shall I flee from thy presence? If I ascen' into 'Eaven, thou h'art there; h'if I makes my bed in 'Ell, thou h'art there h'also. Well, she read it out, an' we say we prayers an' go to bed. Nex' day when de h'eart'quake come, she know what 'appen, an'same day she leave go search fi dem. She ride de whole way from Montego Bay to Kingston, wid Mr Jenkins what did de mason-work for Mass Joe. She beg 'im fi go wid 'ar, an' is a good t'ing, because it tek dem mus' be t'ree days to reach, an' is 'im did 'ave to look place for 'ar to sleep on de road. She tell me when she come back dat is a message she get, to prepare 'ar mind for dem death, an' she never frighten de whole time she was lookin' about dat business. An' same time she mek up 'ar mind dat is she must raise 'ar brother two children, you Daddy an' you h'uncle. So even when time hard, she bring dem up as 'ar own, for she an' Mass Joe never lucky fi raise one of dem own pickney. Is dat mek she almost good fi spoil you h'uncle Eddie, especially as 'im very good lookin' from 'im was a baby, an' if Captain never come an' 'elp 'ar grow de boy, an' sen' de two of dem to study, 'im wouldn' come out to notiing. All de same, 'im never rude an' troublesome like you nowadays pickney! Missis grow dem wid *manners*, an' Captain show dem 'ow dem can 'elp demself, an' do little somet'ing in de world."

Annabell looked at Maud's long, angular face and wondered for the hundredth time how old Maud was (a strictly guarded secret), and if she had been pretty when she was young. Her face could be carved in bone, thought Annabell, looking at the high forehead wrinkled from the way Maud screwed up her brow to stop the inevitable slide of the spectacles down her nose. She peered sharply at Annabell, humming a funny little tune under her breath as the iron went up and down the shirt sleeves and cuffs. The clothes all looked brand new, marvelled Annabell, as she watched napkins, shirts, and towels folded and laid stiff and smooth in the tray. She was sure that she could never get anything as crisp and fresh as that, no matter how hard she tried.

"Practice will make perfect, Miss Anna," said Maud suddenly, as if reading her thoughts. "You can' h'expect fi get what you want overnight. Everyt'ing 'ave a time an' a season, an' you can' run from your time when it come. Me woulda like fi write one letter tell Mr Hitler, for it don' seem like 'im know, poor 'eathen sittin' in darkness."

Chapter Seven

While Annabell was with Maud, Peter had been doing some hard thinking on his own about their problem. It was clear to him that great danger was about to overtake Uncle Simon Peter. He was always in some danger; he had told them so often that the sea is a good servant, but a cruel master. For the first time Peter began to think of what the binoculars were for, and how important they could be in the many chances of seafaring and war. He shivered slightly as he thought of the games they played on the roof, looking for German battleships, they said, while real battleships were shelling each other out at sea, and submarines were searching for merchant ships over the length and breadth of the ocean. When you came out of harbour, you would need your glasses at any moment, for who could tell what was waiting below the horizon? Uncle Simon Peter had explained that the radio did not work well in bad weather; you had to use charts, compass, and perhaps even a pocket watch to help plot your course as you tried to dodge and hide, with a slow engine and a heavy cargo. The nights must be the worst of all, he thought, especially dark, rainy nights with not a star showing, and the useless radio squeaking away like Mickey Mouse. But that was all in the sailor's life, Uncle Simon Peter used to say, like pickled fish and pickled meat and the smell of the sea.

He thought with a sudden cold feeling in his mouth that even as he stood in the sunshine on the verandah at

Virgin Valley, Uncle Simon Peter might be dead, drowned, and floating idly in the waves, his white hair like bleached seaweed, his face as pale as his beard. He shuddered and tried to put the thought out of his mind. But the harder he tried, the more persistent and irresistible the idea became, like the dreadful fascination that fills you for days before an important examination. The idea slinks off when you face it, only to turn up unannounced in a new disguise every five minutes. He called to Dennis and Annabell for another game of dominoes, but they had gone off on affairs of their own, and did not hear him calling. He thought of going to Leebert's, but it was too far to go before lunch, it would make him late and his mother would be cross.

He wandered into the backyard, hesitated near the kitchen door, through which he could overhear Maud telling his sister that corn pork sweeter than corn beef, but it too strong for pickney stomach. No, he did not want to hear about corned anything, and he did not think that the story about Uncle Edwin and the earthquake would be of any use at all. What an idiot Annabell was. Sometimes she was very sensible, for a girl, but she always listened to the rubbish that Maud told her. He climbed the gate into the back paddock, sat absent-mindedly for a while on the top bar, and slid off on the other side. Forgetful of the bull, a half-Brahmin, half-Guernsey personage of changeable temperament, he walked slowly over towards the mound where the cedars towered above the old tombstones. The sun was bright, the bruised grass smelled sweet under his bare toes. He was fingering his Scout knife in his pocket, wondering whether it was worthwhile making a new sling-shot before he left for school in a few days' time. The distant farm sounds floated in the rising wind, mingled with the faint rippling of the cedar trees. Suddenly, it was as if a voice said firmly and clearly in his head: 'Stand still.' He obeyed instinctively, then looked around, so great was his surprise.

Ten feet or so away, behind his left shoulder, between him and the gate and safety, was the lawful tenant of the paddock, looking stupid and angry (which he was), and also rather sleepy (which he wasn't). Peter knew that look; he also noticed with a stab near his heart, that the stiff, ridiculous tail was twitching from side to side in the bushes. All of a sudden Peter felt as if his stomach had fallen out. Why had he come into the paddock? He hadn't really wanted to, and he had forgotten all about Dad's rule that you never went into the paddock without first checking where the bull was. His hands went damp. He wiped them very very slowly on the seat of his pants, never taking his eye off the bull. Its name was Benjie, a name given it by Annabell and Dennis in the long gone days of its youth and innocence, before it became known in the district as 'Missa Ferguson Satan bull'. He wiped his hands again. For a split second his eye left Benje's, and he saw a dry branch lying near him on the ground. It was a small limb chopped off a guava tree, about three feet long. There was a sharp, slanting edge to it where the machete had severed it. The same voice said in his head, 'Pick it up, slowly.' Sweat ran down his face as he bent very slowly and grasped the piece of wood. As his fingers closed on it he felt a little better, and then much worse as the movement attracted Benjie's morose attention. He had trouble straightening his shaking knees. He thought, "What am I to do now?"

The thought of Uncle Simon Peter came back to him, for no particular reason, it seemed to him. He saw him clearly in his mind for an instant, and for that fraction of a second his attention was completely disengaged from the danger he was in. Then the voice said for the third and last time, 'Point the stick at his face and walk backwards.' He raised the branch with both hands, trying to keep it steady, and took one slow step backwards. Benjie's eyes remained fixed on him. He stopped breathing. After what seemed an age he took another step and waited. He almost fell over with the effort of holding the stick firm and keeping his own balance. Another step. Benjie snorted. He froze. Then he saw that Benjie's tail was hanging almost limp. Another step, another, and another. Benjie shook his head, and Peter froze again. They were now about fifteen feet apart. The nearest tomb, that of Ezekiel Martin, was about fifty feet away. How he crossed that patch of open field, Peter always shuddered to remember. Benjie watched him go with a mixture of uncertainty and loathing. He tossed his head at flies and snorted several times. Each time the bull moved, Peter's heart leaped up in his throat with a bump. He felt sick but he never took his eye off the bull, or turned to run, not even when he stumbled against the root of the nearest cedar tree. Only when at last he struck his back on the tomb did he turn and leap with all his strength on to the high brick tombstone. All in the same movement he threw himself at the trunk of the overhanging cedar and shinned up the stout trunk like a monkey, leaving a lot of skin behind on the rough bark.

He was astride the lowest limb, a safe ten feet above the ground, when he paused to catch his breath and look down.

Benjie had followed him slowly but purposefully across the field, and was even then scraping his huge

Died on the
November

sides against the tomb as he searched for his enemy. The guava stick lay on the ground by the tomb, and snapped like a match-stick as Benjie trod on it in his search for Peter. Then he looked up and saw him, and an expression of bewildered, frustrated malice crept into the staring eyes. Benjie was not known for the sweetness of his temper. He gave vent to his emotions in the best way he knew: he bellowed and stamped. He humped his way around the tree, sometimes hitting himself on the tombstones, which he seemed not to notice. Then he began to paw the ground under Peter's tree, and soon had a large patch of bare earth to show for his pains. He had stopped bellowing, and Peter had begun to hope that he had forgotten about him, and would soon wander away. Then, to Peter's surprise, the bull did not go away; it turned around carefully and urinated on the patch it had made, turning the loose earth to mud. Peter noticed that Benjie was standing still in an unnatural way, swinging his tail from side to side in a gentle curve, then faster and wider. Before he had time to think what this could mean, a splash of horrible, nasty mud struck the tree trunk just below him, and before he could move his legs were splashed too. It itched dreadfully, and he had to climb up as high as he dared to get away from the menace. When Benjie saw him climb higher, he gave another bellow; but he did not move away.

It was nearly an hour later that Dennis, sent by Mrs Ferguson to search for Peter, heard a warning shout from high up in the cedar trees, and saw Benjie on guard by Ezekiel Martin's grave. It took Leebert, Charlie, and two other men to drive him off, and Mrs Ferguson was so frightened that she sent Peter to bed in disgrace for the rest of the day. Dennis narrowly escaped a spanking for laughing at his brother, and an atmosphere of gloom hung over the house in the afternoon.

Peter was allowed out of bed at supper-time, mainly because the tailor, Mr Simmons, had brought Peter's new school blazer for a last fitting. At a signal from Peter the three children went up early to bed, much to their mother's relief. She might have felt a little different had she overheard the conversation that took place upstairs. Peter was telling the other two that Uncle Simon Peter must be in danger; submarines were coming closer and closer, and some were already in the Caribbean. He had seen a report in the *Daily Gleaner* which said that German submarines had attacked Port-of-Spain in Trinidad, and had even been sighted off Kingston harbour. The *Freya* was in constant peril.

"They might even follow her into harbour at Montego Bay and torpedo her in there!" he exclaimed: a terrible idea suddenly seizing him. "If Aunt Flossie knew–"

"Do you really think the Germans could come into the harbour and sink Uncle Simon Peter's ship?" asked Dennis in a small voice.

"Of course they could! Easy as cheese!" Peter answered. "We *have* to do something for him. We *have* to. Aunt Flossie would have done something if she was still alive. She wouldn't sit down and let things happen to him!"

He stole a look at Annabell, standing silent beside the untidy chest of drawers.

"What do you think, Annabell?" Peter's voice was urgent.

"I asked Maud." Peter nodded, and Annabell went on slowly. "I think– I think we must do something like what she did, when she heard about Grandpa and Grandma, and Great Uncle Joe. Maud told me."

A little while later the three children were seated in a circle in the middle of Annabell's bed. They were supposed to be asleep, and two dummies made of pillows and towels had been carefully assembled in the boys' beds, in case their mother looked in on them on her way to bed. The door of Annabell's room was shut, and a canopy had been erected over the bed, consisting of the mosquito-net and the top sheet. This tent was illuminated by a jarful of peeni-wallies, which shed a restless, greenish light over the still figures of the children. For once there was no giggling or pinching. The dark faces of Annabell and Peter melted in the gloom, but Peter's eyes shone bright. Dennis was a small grey shadow beside them, his breathing loud in the narrow space of the tent.

"How shall we do it, Peter?" whispered Annabell hoarsely. She was holding Great Aunt Flossie's chain in her hands. On the bed in the middle was the little boat which Uncle Simon Peter had given them on his last visit. Peter was holding the binoculars in one hand, and Dennis had taken the compass from its box.

"Put everything down beside the ship, and hold hands," he ordered.

"Must we shut our eyes?" asked Dennis, sounding rather scared.

"No – Yes, I suppose so. You don't have to be frightened, it's just like saying our prayers. Well, it is really saying prayers, isn't it? It's all we can do now, really. Annabell, where's the Bible?"

"Here. Wait; Dennis, you're sitting on it! I marked the place, Peter, but I can't see to read it out properly, the print is so small. Why didn't you get the big Bible

from the drawing-room? This print is as fine as ants' feet." She peered at the page crossly.

"All right, let *me* read it, then," said Peter, taking the book from her. "I'm closer to the light, and anyway your eyes look as if they're going to jump out of your head."

Annabell passed the open Bible to Peter, who told them to put the compass, watch, and binoculars together with the ship, and hold hands.

"What about you?" asked Dennis. "You can't read and hold hands at the same time! And I don't suppose it's any good if we aren't all holding hands, is it?"

There was some fussing and shuffling around, and then Annabell put a pillow in front of Peter, and set the Bible on that, with the jar of peenies right beside it so that Peter could see well enough to do the reading. Then they held hands, the younger two closed their eyes, and Peter began.

Together they said the prayer they always said at bedtime, Peter's voice leading the other two:

"Now the day is over,
   Night is drawing nigh,
Shadows of the evening
   Steal across the sky.

Jesu, give the weary
   Calm and sweet repose;
With thy tenderest blessing
   May my eyelids close.

Grant to little children
   Visions bright of thee;
Guard the sailor tossing
   On the angry sea.

When the morning wakens,
Then may I arise
Pure and fresh and sinless
In thy holy eyes.

Dennis did not know some of the verses in the middle as well as the others did, and stumbled over the words once or twice. Then they opened their eyes and Peter blinked at the dark pages of the little school Bible open before him.

"I'm going to read all of it," he said, "because that is what Aunt Flossie did. Annabell, you''ll have to turn the page for me."

He cleared his throat and began reading softly and clearly, even though he felt embarrassed at the sound of his own voice going on and on all alone while the others watched him.

"Psalm One Hundred and Thirty-nine," said Peter, screwing up his eyes to see better.

"O Lord thou hast searched me and known me.
Thou knowest my down-sitting and mine uprising, thou understandest my thought afar off.
Thou compassest my path and my lying down, and art acquainted with all my ways.
For there is not a word in my tongue, but, lo, O Lord, thou knowest it altogether."

Dennis began to fidget and Annabell squeezed his hand sharply as Peter's voice read on in the heavy stillness.

"Whither shall I go from thy spirit? or whither shall I flee from thy presence?
If I ascend into heaven, thou art there: if I make my bed in hell, thou art there.
If I take the wings of the morning, and dwell in the uttermost parts of the sea;
Even there shall thy hand lead me, and thy right

hand shall hold me."

Annabell's hand shook a little as she let go Dennis's hand and turned the page for Peter. He read right on to the end, even though it was a long psalm, full of things which none of them understood properly, like "thou hast possessed my reins", which made them think of harness and bridles, and also a great deal about the wicked, which reminded Peter of the submarines searching for the *Freya*, while Dennis thought of one of the boys who teased him at school, and Annabell remembered the last time she had been nasty to Dennis, and was sorry.

Peter finished reading and they shut their eyes again. Now it was Annabell's turn.

"Please God," she began in a small voice, holding tightly to her brothers' hands. "We think you want us to do something to help Uncle Simon Peter, something that Aunt Flossie thinks is very important. Please, we are ready to do it, whatever it is. But we don't know what we are supposed to do, and when we are to do it. So we are trying to keep ready all the time from now on, so that we'll be ready for it, no matter what. If we are to give up something, we are willing. If we are to do something special, please help us to do it properly. And thank you for everything, most of all yourself, though we don't understand properly. Amen."

They opened their eyes and blinked at one another.

"Well," said Peter. "We've done it. And we'll do it every night we three are together, until he comes home safe and sound. I'm sure Aunt Flossie would agree. She's not going to like it if anything happens to him out there." He waved a hand northwards, where the dark seas broke on the beaches of St. James and Trelawny.

Six days later, Mr and Mrs Ferguson took Peter on

the bus to Montego Bay for his first term at high school, and the opportunity of celebrating his thirteenth birthday away from home, with only the promise of a card from Annabell and Dennis to cheer him up. It seemed very hard, especially as his birthday fell on a Tuesday, which meant that most of it would be wasted sitting in a class room among boys he had never met. But he had proper pocket money for the first time in his life, and Dad said that Uncle Edwin would come and see him at Miss French's, so perhaps life was not too bad after all.

Chapter Eight

Peter started his new life at high school in what were perhaps the darkest times of the war. In the early months of 1942 he had to face new teachers, new text books, new rules and new friends, and though he soon got used to Miss French, and made several friends both at school and at the boarding-house, there were times when he was very homesick. Also Montego Bay had always meant Uncle Simon Peter, and this time everything was different. There was no one at the house on Barnet Street but the elderly couple who rented half of the house from Uncle Simon Peter. He did not like them very much, so he did not visit Barnet Street. And now that he was actually living in Montego Bay himself, the war seemed very much closer, and far more real than it had before. To begin with, everyone at Cornwall College seemed to be thinking and talking of nothing else. The harbour was off-limits, black-outs

were practised, and there was actually a military post in the town. Miss French insisted that all of her boarders listen to the news on the big old battery radio in the living room. Dance music was forbidden, but she expected them to know all of the latest news, and to be able to say what was the state of the fighting in what she referred to as 'the theatres of war'. The two Fifth Form boarders had an enormous map of the world pinned up in the dining room, and on it were arrayed not simply pins representing different countries, but tacks tagged with coloured paper to represent armoured divisions, aircraft, convoys, and submarines. It looked very professional to Peter, thinking of the globe at home with its dozen coloured pins borrowed from his mother's sewing basket. Then there was the cadet corps, to which the two Fifth Formers belonged. Even the Lower Fourth, Peter's form, was wholly addicted to war comics and spy stories, in which dare-devil pilots flew impossible missions over the Himalayas or into the heart of Germany, and commando units fought their way through jungle, tundra, desert, or steppe to overcome the enemy with acts of incredible heroism and luck. A feud destined to last as long as the war developed between Lower Four A and Lower Four B as to which was better: the army or the air-force. Peter considered the navy to be better than either, himself; that is, if he had had to choose, he would have chosen the navy. But he felt the choices were stupid (what Uncle Simon Peter would have called nonsense), and he stayed on the fringes of the debate.

Meanwhile gas rationing was threatened, and Peter's weekends at home might never be possible. He did his homework at Cornwall College in nasty little exercise books half the size of those he had had the year before.

The pages were soft and made blotches when you wrote on them in ink. Very often mail disappeared forever, either on some ship torpedoed at sea, or in a Post Office bombed in England. The history and algebra books for the Fourth Forms did not arrive; second-hand copies had to be scraped together by borrowing from the older boys, and making appeals through the Old Boys' Association. And hardly a week passed at school when the headmaster did not announce the departure for England or Canada of some Old Boy who was off to join the air-force or the army.

But it was at Miss French's that Peter felt the worst effects of the war in Montego Bay; or, that is how Miss French explained the size and composition of the meals which she set before her twelve starving boarders. They had beef stew on Sundays in a thin grey gravy that looked as if it came straight from Barnet River; Mondays was hash, different only in the prevalence of carrots and the darker brown of the gravy. Tuesdays was fried fish, which was the best of all, but there was never enough. On Wednesdays they got curried eggs and were told they were lucky. Thursdays was stew-peas, and was the only day when anyone rose from the table feeling satisfied. Fridays was always macaroni-cheese, which Peter loathed, and on Saturdays they had boiled oxheart or liver. There were no second helpings. Desserts consisted of a ripe banana or half a grapefruit. Breakfast was always the same: cornmeal porridge, cocoa, and two slices of brown bread with margarine. Miss Frenh reminded them constantly that thousands of people in the world were dying of starvation, and would be glad for half of what they had on their plates. It is not surprising that apart from the war, food was the main topic of conversation at the boarding house. Very soon

Peter had become a regular client of the bakery that turned out 'Regal Biscuits', a jaw-breaking, tooth-splitting biscuit as big as a plate and as hard as rock. But that meant that pocket-money had to be carefully saved.

He came home for his first weekend visit in the middle of February, and almost cried when the Virgin Valley house came into view. He was driven over by a friend of Uncle Edwin's who worked with the Public Works, and was making a tour of inspection of roads and bridges in that part of St. James. He would have to get up very early on Monday morning to get a lift on a truck going to Montego Bay for goods, but he preferred the prospect of being roused at 4.00 a.m. by his father, and walking down the dark drive all by himself to meet the truck on the main road, to that of spending a Sunday evening at the boarding house.

The three children had a lot to talk about when Peter arrived on Friday night. At first Dennis and Annabell felt shy of him; he looked suddenly grown-up in his school uniform with its shoulder-straps and badge. It made him look taller too. But as soon as he had torn off socks and shoes (a matter of seconds), and had flung his school bag in a corner of the living room, and then had turned two cartwheels in the backyard, they were all quite at ease together again.

It was too late to go up on the roof, so they compromised by sitting on the outside landing where they could talk undisturbed. Dennis and Annabell had to hear all about the boarding house, the other boys there, and what it was like going to a big high school for boys. Peter found it rather hard to explain about form captains, detentions, and prefects, for none of them was really interested in all that. They were much more keen on hearing about the movie to which Uncle Edwin took him on the Saturday after his birthday. Miss French had given permission most reluctantly, but he had had a marvellous time, and had eaten several patties and three ice-cream cones, and had seen a wonderful musical with Nelson Eddy called *Rose Marie*. It was all about the Canadian Mounted Police, and he could sing two of the songs. Annabell made him promise to get the words and music for her. Then he told them all about the military camp in Montego Bay, and how he had gone with some friends from school to watch them drilling. You had to climb a tree in the open land that overlooked the camp ground, but it was well worth it, red ants and all. The soldiers in the camp were English or Canadian, he was not sure which, and they had real guns and armoured cars. They were a detachment from the military base at Up Park Camp in Kingston, where the British regiments on duty in the West Indies were customarily stationed.

Annabell and Dennis felt very countrified and left out. All they had to report was that Benjie had been moved to another paddock, and that some boys from school had played a trick on old Mr Obadiah Evans from Cedar Hill, a small farmer of legendary meanness, much disliked by all school children who had ever been driven away from his plum trees. As everyone knew, old Mr Evans never let his wife buy the family groceries, and doled out the produce of his farm with great reluctance. He preferred to spend his days down at his field, where he kept a cache of food, and cooked himself enormous lunches in a kerosene tin big enough to serve for ten men.

"Well, remember how scared he is of Germans?" asked Dennis, who had had the full story from Mervyn

Griffiths, one of the criminals. "He's always saying that the Germans are coming, and he's going to be bombed in his house any night!"

Peter nodded. He remembered the plum trees only too well. He also knew that Mr Evans was the one person in Somerton who lived in daily expectation of air-raids and invasion. Dennis went on to tell that a group of Sixth Class boys were sent one Friday to cut sticks for the yams in the school garden, and came upon Mr Evans in his field with the hug tin of food steaming temptingly over a small fire.

"Missa Evans! Missa Evans!" they shouted in shrill, scared voices. "Missa Evans! Missa Evans! Bumb drap a Samatan! Bumb drap a Samatan! Come quick before you 'ouse burn down!"

Off he ran, throwing away machete and fork in his panic, and covering the two miles to his house in about ten minutes. He came back an hour later to find the kerosene tin carefully washed out and turned down in the shade, and a note saying 'Thanks for the lunch. Adolf Hitler'. Even though all of those involved got into fearful trouble at school, and had to do a day's work each with Mr Evans to make up, it was well worth it. Mr Evans had started to have lunch at home with his wife, and he had to buy drinks all round at the bar at Cross Roads to stop the giggles and remarks that began as soon as he entered.

"What about Uncle Simon Peter?" asked Peter when they had all stopped laughing.

Annabell's face fell.

"Dad hasn't had a letter from him since you left. Has Uncle Edwin heard from him?"

Peter shook his head, and all three children were silent. That night they carried out their secret ceremony again, and Peter slept with the little ship beside his pillow. No news had come from Uncle Simon Peter since his visit in November, and their mother said brightly that perhaps a letter was delayed somewhere, they were sure to hear soon. But she did not like to talk about it, and turned the conversation whenever the children asked anything about him.

The weekend went too fast for Peter. It seemed to have been no time at all before he was packing again, helped by his mother, and telling Annabell and Dennis goodbye. His father gave him a letter to Miss French, giving him unlimited permission to go out with Uncle Edwin, and to come home every fortnight provided that he (Peter) could find reliable transportation home and back. His mother gave him five shillings pocket-money, and Maud a box of her special chocolate fudge.

Annabell and Dennis felt even duller and more miserable after Peter's visit. Now that they had been told all about the excitements of life in Montego Bay (barring Miss French's hostel), they felt left out and depressed. Annabell was sent to take extra lessons from the Fifth Class teacher, Miss Webster, and that was all. Both of them started to give trouble in class and were reported to their parents. They missed Peter far more than he missed them; all their games had been worked out for three, and he had been the big brother who could do the hard things that Dennis was too small to manage, or the nasty things that upset Annabell. They could not get on without him. Their parents noticed the squabbling and restlessness, and guessed what was wrong.

At the beginning of March Annabell came down with a bad cold. She was kept in bed for two days, felt much better, and went wading in the spring with

Dennis when both Maud and their mother were at the market in Somerton. By evening she had a high fever and a heavy weight in her chest, as though her lungs were full of lead. The district nurse came to see her, and that same night Mrs Ferguson took Annabell wrapped in blankets down to the main road in the buggy, where they got a lift into Montego Bay from a passing car. Annabell was admitted to hospital with pneumonia, and Mrs Ferguson spent the night in a chair by the bed holding her hands and seeing nothing but the thin dark face on the pillow.

Next morning Mrs Ferguson went to Barnet Street to explain to the tenants, Mr and Mrs Edwards, that she would be occupying Uncle Simon Peter's rooms for the time being, as Annabell was in hospital very ill. They were only too pleased to have her to stay, and would have loved to hear every detail of Annabell's illness, if Mrs Ferguson had had the energy or the inclination to satisfy their anxious curiosity. She dozed on the four-poster bed upstairs for an hour, and was back at the hospital before the doctor finished his rounds.

"Can you send for her Aunt Flossie?" asked the doctor. "I hear that she got very excited after you left, and began to call for her. She must be kept as quiet as possible, you know, and we're doing everything possible."

"But–" began Mrs Ferguson, looking troubled.

The doctor cut her short.

"No time for buts, Mrs Ferguson. Your little girl is very ill, and you look pretty worn out yourself. Get this Aunt to come and sit with her; it'll help a lot, mark my word." And he hurried away before she could get a word in.

Annabell got worse that day. Even her mother, who

was a brave and optimistic person, could see that. In the afternoon Mrs Ferguson begged a nurse going off duty to send a telegram to Somerton summoning her husband. She did not eat or rest for the remainder of that day. Annabell seemed to fall in and out of a half-sleep, sometimes moaning quietly, sometimes muttering in her sleep. When evening came her fever rose higher, and she no longer recognised her mother. She kept on saying, "What are we to do, Aunt Flossie? What are we to *do*?"

Mrs Ferguson tried to talk to her and reassure her. She told her not to worry, mother was here. But Annabell's glance slid uncomprehendingly over her, and a little while later she would ask for Aunt Flossie again. This was the state of affairs when Mr Ferguson arrived, having ridden his horse Jenny over short-cuts and bridle-tracks to Montego Bay where Mrs Edwards told him that Annabell was dying, and his wife still at the hospital even though it was nearly eight o'clock at night.

Annabell herself knew little of all this, and cared less. She knew she was in hospital, but she was no longer certain how she had got there, or why, or how long it was since she had been brought into the children's ward. Her mother was there, but she could not get her to understand that they must find out what Aunt Flossie wanted them to do. Instead they kept giving her tablets to swallow, that hurt going down, and tried to force her to drink things she did not want. She grew tired of telling them that all she needed was to have Aunt Flossie come and explain to her just how to help Uncle Simon Peter. Then her mother left. Annabell hoped she had gone for Aunt Flossie, which should be quite easy since they were in Montego Bay anyway. She was sure of *that*, and Barnet Street wasn't far away. If her head did not swim so much, and if her eyes did not hurt so when she moved, she would go and ask her herself. The nurses hurt her when they raised her in the bed. All of her seemed to ache and the weight in her chest became a suffocating force drawing her down, down, down into a restless, troubled dark where the sea roared, storm-winds flowed in the frozen night, and Uncle Simon Peter's laugh echoed from somewhere both far away and near enough for her to reach if she kept on trying.

All through the night she kept trying to get nearer to the place from which the voice came. Sometimes she could hear him quite plainly, talking to someone on board the *Freya*, but she could not make out what he was saying. Then he seemed to be at Virgin Valley, explaining to them about steering by the stars, and that was certainly odd, but then her father came into the room, so she must be up at Virgin Valley after all. But then he disappeared too, and a nurse came with another glass of water and more pills to be swallowed, and told her to be a good girl and have them at once. If she had not been so angry with them for not calling Aunt Flossie for her, she would have burst into tears; but then she overheard Uncle Simon Peter saying quite distinctly to Peter and Dennis that "You must yust turn this part here, so and so, and the focus is clear and sharp. Very good glasses they are, though older than your mother!" And he chuckled.

So Annabell knew nothing at all of the events of that night and the following day, when her father sent Uncle Edwin down to Somerton to bring back Maud and Dennis, and such clothes and other necessities as Mrs Ferguson had been unable to bring with her. She did not even know that her father sat by her bed all of the next day, nodding in his chair, while her mother rested at the house on Barnet Street. And she did not realise that she had been moved out of the ward during the night into a private room kept for desperately ill patients, or for those needing relatively little care. It was a room overlooking the sea, and the noise of the breakers falling on the rocks below could be plainly heard. But Annabell was asleep at last, and she would have heard the whistle of the wind only through her sleep. The doctor looked more cheerful, but still shook his head and pursed his lips when Mr Ferguson questioned him.

Dennis arrived in Montego Bay that morning, nervous and confused. He had been terrified from the evening before by the telegram which came just when he got home from school, and he had had his supper with Maud and slept that night with her in the brass bed. Nothing could persuade him to go upstairs. But in the morning he was scolded and packed off to school, and told not to be a coward. At school he felt a little better, but he kept forgetting where he was, and what he was supposed to be doing. His teacher, who had not been told that Annabell was in hospital, took a poor view of this and sent him outside after first recess to sit by the headmaster's office and copy out the first six verses of Longfellow's 'Excelsior'.

Suddenly the attention of every child in the school was riveted by the sound of a motor vehicle roaring down the stony little road that led to the school. Dennis had a good view from his bench outside Mr Creary's office.

It was Uncle Edwin.

In a trice he was told to get his books together and climb into the van. Then, while the envious eyes of three hundred and fifteen children watched the lucky one who had been released from decimals, spelling tests, and memory gems for the day, they drove out of the schoolyard in a cloud of dust.

"How's Annabell, Uncle Edwin?" Dennis was asking in a trembly voice. He connected hospitals invariably with death, having heard hideous stories at school about people who took sick suddenly and died in hospital the same day.

"Not too bad," lied Uncle Edwin, who had seen the wide eyes turned towards him. "But she can't come home yet. Your Dad doesn't want you to stay alone at home, and they'd forgotten to take enough clothes for themselves. So you're going to spend a little holiday in MoBay for the rest of this week, or until the doctor says Annabell can come home. Maud's packing up now, and your job is to find some books for your sister to read when she feels better, and bring them along with whatever you want for yourself."

Dennis let his breath out quietly and concentrated on studying the trees and fence-posts flipping by. He forgot about Annabell and began pestering his uncle to let him hold the steering-wheel, *just* a little, please?

When they arrived at the house, Maud called out that Leebert was waiting to see Uncle Edwin, and would somebody please come and take the luggage out to the van? Dennis dashed off to his room and then to Annabell's. He dug quickly through the clothes in the bureau, and found the watch. Then he gathered up the boat, the compass, and the binoculars, remembered about the books and dragged three at random off the topshelf of the children's bookcase in the passage. Emptying his schoolbag on the floor of his room, he carefully put in the watch, the compass, the binoculars, and the three books. The boat was too big to hold, so he carried that in his hands. Then he remembered a pack of cards belonging to Peter, and Annabell's Japanese dolls, and took those too. The horn blew from the front door, and he ran downstairs with his bag and the ship clutched to his chest. Uncle Edwin and Leebert were putting the small black tin-case, a market basket, and the large brown tin-case in the back of the van. Maud, in her best dress, was calling to him to get in at once and not keep them waiting. He climbed breathlessly on to the seat beside her, and they set off.

Chapter Nine

Dennis alone of the three children did not remember living at Barnet Street. Aunt Flossie had died before his second birthday, and he had been to Barnet Street only on rare occasions when Uncle Simon Peter was delayed in Montego Bay and could not come up to Virgin Valley. Dennis loved the verandahs at the house on Barnet Street, especially the wide, cool upstairs verandah, with its rocking chairs, its fish tank, and the great pots of ferns, geraniums, and violets. There was also an enormous lily in a tub that stood higher than Dennis himself. The rooms were higher and dimmer than those at Virgin Valley, and were painted in pale shades of blue and green instead of the plain cream wash he was used to. The doors had shiny brass handles like the knobs on Maud's bed, but none of these compared to the joys of the bathroom upstairs, with its vast tiled bathtub ('as big as a swimming pool,' he thought); its rim came almost up to his chest, and when he sat in it and stretched out his arms, his fingers just managed to brush the two sides. What was marvellous, too, was the low window that opened right above the bath, so that you could sit in the tub and (if you were the size of Uncle Simon Peter) you could look over the roofs of the houses behind Barnet Street all the way down to the warehouses along the bay.

Dennis hoped that Annabell would be out of hospital and waiting for them at Barnet Street. They would have a great time together.

But when Uncle Edwin stopped the van in Barnet Street, old Mr Edwards hurried out to tell them that both Mamma and Dad were at the hospital, and that Annabell was very ill indeed. Mrs Edwards appeared on the scene wiping her hands hastily on a dish-towel. Maud did not like either of them, because they had committed the great crime of living in Missis and Captain house, where no human being except Mr Joe or Mr Edwin had any right to be. Fear for Annabell alone made her civil to the Edwards. Her glasses misted over as she called sharply to Dennis to mind his manners and help her carry their luggage inside. The Edwards fussed and fussed, giving contradictory instructions and advice, and could not be got rid of. Uncle Edwin said he had to get back to work, but he would return in the evening. He pinched Dennis's arm very hard, and drove off with a squeal of tyres.

During the afternoon Mr and Mrs Ferguson came home to rest and eat. Dennis was told to get ready to accompany one or other of them to the hospital, for Annabell was a little better and had been asking for both him and Peter. He set off an hour later with his father for the long walk to the hospital.

"Now remember to be quiet," admonished Mr Ferguson as they came within sight of the white gates of the hospital. "Annabell will be glad to see you, but you mustn't get her excited".

"Where is she Dad?" asked Dennis, hesitating at the main entrance. He hated the hospital smell of antiseptic, carbolic soap, and dishwater soup, mingled as this was with faint, nameless odours of a most unsettling kind. He wanted to get away as fast as he could.

"She's up here, in a room by herself. Overlooking the sea." He looked down at Dennis for a moment. "You'll like that."

Annabell was sitting propped up in bed when they arrived, being fed a glass of milk by a young nurse with a cheerful grin. She brightened as they came in, and her father was rewarded with a shaky smile. Mr Ferguson took the glass from the nurse, saying that Annabell would not refuse to have another sip, just for his sake.

"Well do try with her, sir." The nurse smiled and moved to close the door. "She'll drink if you ask her to, I'm sure. But this young man mustn't be noisy, or he'll have to leave!"

She patted him on the head and said how pretty his hair was. Annabell caught his eye and almost giggled, but she drank all of the milk to please her father, who left shortly after to go in search of the doctor. The wind came fresh off the sea, and the pounding of the waves below was louder than ever. As he left, Mr Ferguson cautioned Dennis to keep the door to Annabell's room shut, and then he hurried off.

"All of us are staying round at Barnet Street," began Dennis. "Guess what! Uncle Edwin came and took me right out of school this morning, after recess, and a good thing too!" he added darkly, recalling Longfellow and the bench outside Mr Creary's office.

"Brought anything for me?" asked Annabell hopefully. She had no idea what she wanted, but felt it would be nice to have *something*: anything bright and cheerful that would help her forget the strange, nightmarish memories of the last two days and nights.

"Oh gosh!" Dennis dug hastily into his pockets. "I nearly forgot! I brought *everything*."

He held out his hand and dropped a little blue box in Annabell's lap.

"I've wound it up for you, and Uncle Edwin set it off his watch."

Annabell's fingers closed weakly on the box.

"At least you'll know what time it is. What a way it's dark and ugly in here!" He glanced with dislike at the plain white-washed room with its dark green blind and grey concrete floor.

But Annabell was not listening to him. She lifted out the silver chain and let the links glide through her fingers.

"It is *really* pretty," she said, half to herself. "I wouldn't like anything to happen to it."

"Oh! And I have the telescope" (Dennis could never be persuaded to say binoculars) "I brought that and the compass and the ship and all! We can look out from this window and see everything coming into the harbour, Annabell!"

But Annabell was absorbed in letting the long chain slip round and round her hand, pulled down by the weight of the boars' heads with their staring eyes.

"I wonder what they're staring at so hard?" she murmured. She seemed drowsy and far-away, and after a while Dennis left her dozing on the bed and went in search of his father, braving the horrors of the hospital corridor.

He walked timidly down the corridor in the direction taken by his father. Nurses and porters passed him by, busy with their work. One of the senior sisters stared at him and said, "visiting hours are up!"

He was afraid of getting lost, afraid of being stopped and questioned, afraid of seeing something dreadful in any of the rooms he passed, afraid of being ordered off the premises before he found his father. Unknown to him, Mr Ferguson was at that moment sitting in the Matron's office enjoying a much-needed cup of tea. The Matron was telling him that Annabell might be well enough to leave hospital in another two days, but only because they knew she would be staying in Montego Bay near by, and would be very carefully nursed at home.

Dennis went miles up and down various corridors, it seemed to him; finally he decided that it was no good, he couldn't find his father, he had better go back to Annabell's room and wait. He managed to find his way there without mishap, but the smells of the hospital were beginning to make him feel rather sick. At Annabell's door he paused. Annabell was lying on her side fast asleep. It was growing dark in the room, but no lights had been turned on anywhere. He closed the door carefully behind him, and sat down on the hard little chair by the bed to wait.

It had been a long day for Dennis, and he had not slept well the night before. Presently his eyes began to burn, and he yawned once or twice. He wished his father would come back. But though occasional footsteps could be heard passing along the corridor outside, no one came in. It grew darker, and he began to nod. Strangely enough, he was not frightened, and he had forgotten all about feeling sick. He was only very, very sleepy. He leaned his head against the side of the bed. The sea roared on the rocks below, with its unceasing crash of waves.

How long he dozed he did not know, but he was vaguely aware after a while that someone had entered the room, and was laughing quietly. He struggled to open his eyes, and felt a pair of hands lifting him on to the bed. 'So Dad must have come back,' he thought sleepily, making a great effort to wake up properly. He held on to the arm around his shoulders and climbed on to the foot of the bed. Annabell was still fast asleep.

But as he turned around to sit on the bed, he came wide awake. In the dimness he could see that this was not his father at all, nor even one of the nurses. A tall, elderly lady was bending over Annabell, pulling the covers over her shoulders. There was a sharp, sweet scent in the room, a piercing freshness that made his throat go tight for an instant. He wondered vaguely who she was, and then was too sleepy to think about it further. The bed felt so very, very smooth under his tired arms and legs. He felt she was a very nice person, whoever she was. That was all that mattered. He curled up at the foot of the bed and went to sleep at once.

And that was where his father and the night nurse found him, dead to the world, some time later. Annabell was fast asleep too, a mild sweat on her brow and her breath smooth and regular for the first time in four days. They had great trouble rousing Dennis to take him home. He seemed confused and stupid, and his father decided not to bring him back for any more visits. He could stay at Barnet Street instead and plague Maud all day. Next morning when his mother told him

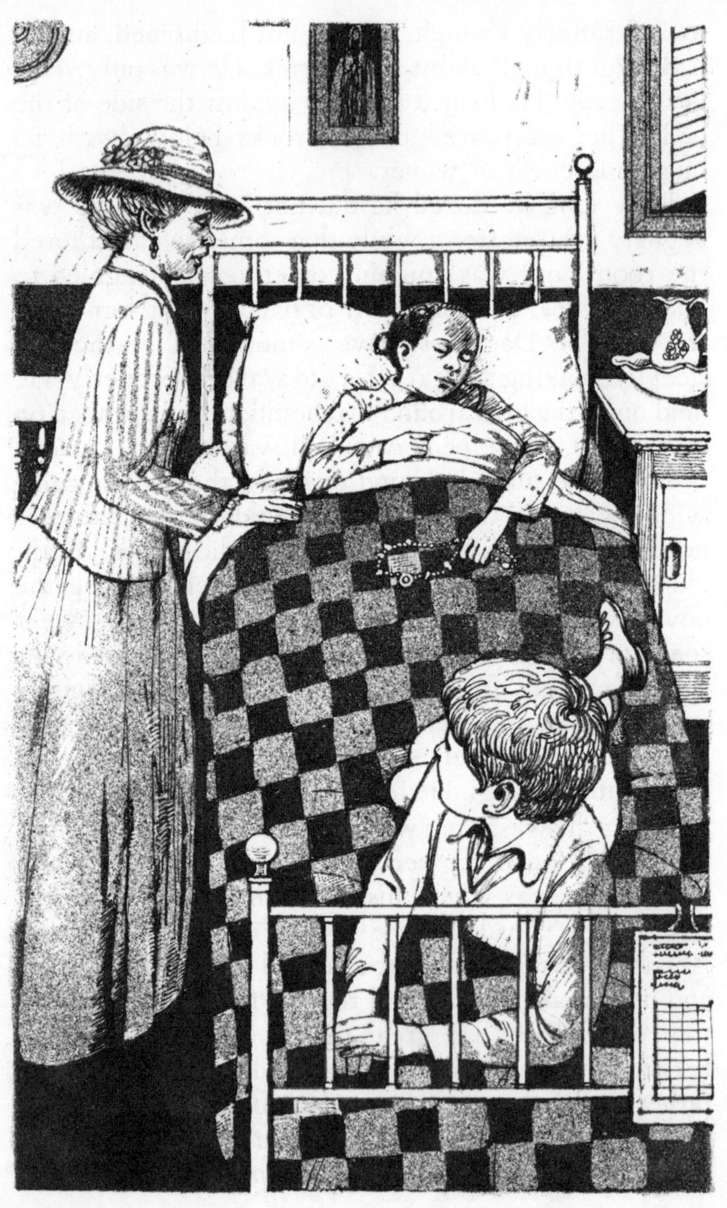

that Annabell was getting better and might leave hospital in a day or two, he only said, "Oh yes, I know. Can I go and look for Peter today?" His mother sighed, and his father replied that they would see Peter soon enough.

Dennis spent the rest of the day upstairs. He filled the great bath-tub with water and tried out the model ship in it. He was pleased to discover that it floated well, and seemed impenetrable by water. He begged an empty shoe-polish tin from Mrs Edwards, scrubbed it carefully, dried it, and tested it to see if it would leak. It did not. He balanced it on the foredeck of the little boat, and noticed that the load made little difference to the bouyancy of the boat, so next he tied it on firmly with string, and made waves in the tub to see what would happen. He made quite a lot of noise as well as waves, but by the time Maud came upstairs to stop him, he had completed his experiments to his satisfaction, and was innocently watching the last of the water gurgle down the plug hole of the tub.

"Patient Saviour 'ear my cry!" exclaimed Maud at the bathroom door. "Is what you doin' in 'ere h'all day? You not satisfy dat you sister gone to 'ospital, is dere you want fi go too? Come downstairs come talk to you bredda, 'im come from school come look fi you–"

But Dennis was down the stairs already.

Peter had to go back to Miss French's after supper, but the boys managed to have a secret conference on the upstairs verandah. The house on Barnet Stret had many nooks, corners, and odd hiding-places where people could go to be alone, they discovered. The best place was in the angle of the verandah behind the great pot of lilies, where you could squeeze in between the flower pots and be quite hidden from anyone coming along the verandah.

As soon as they had crept in between the railings and the screen of ferns and lily leaves, Dennis said in an excited whisper, "I think I've seen Aunt Flossie!"

As he hoped, Peter's face lit up with surprise.

"You can't! You don't know her!" cried Peter, feeling cross because he was a little jealous of Dennis, free from the shackles of school and staying at Barnet Street while he had to be back at nasty old Miss French's by eight o'clock sharp.

"Well, it must have been Aunt Flossie." Dennis sounded doubtful, and much less pleased. "I never asked anybody who she was. I just thought she was somebody who had come to see Annabell. It wasn't until this morning that I thought about it, and then there was a message–" his voice trailed off. "I fell asleep on Annabell's bed, waiting for Dad. Maybe I dreamt it all. But she says that Uncle Simon Peter needs his glasses and the compass, badly. She says we're to send them for him, and you will know how to do it."

He stared at Peter, looking worried.

"Tell me again, all of it," said Peter, feeling contrite. "Never mind who you think this person is, just tell me as it happened."

So bit by bit, with many interruptions from Peter, he told how he had gone to see Annabell, and had given her the watch, because he thought she would like to have it. Then she became tired and drowsy, and he went off to search for Dad all over the hospital and nearly got lost. Then he had gone back to the room and dozed in the chair, only waking up when someone started to lift him on to the foot of the bed.

"I didn't go up there myself, he insisted. "This lady was there, and she helped me. But, but it was dark, you know, and all they have are those funny little blue bulbs burning in the passage."

He could give no real description of the lady, but kept repeating that she was very nice, he liked her, and she smelt very nice, too. No, he couldn't say what her dress was like; it was too dark to see. "But she loves jokes!" he added suddenly, and then could not explain why he said that.

"Well, either she told me, or else I dreamt it, but she *did* say that Uncle Simon Peter needs the telescope and compass, and you will know how to send them!" he added defiantly.

Peter was silent for a while. Then he asked,

"What did you say the perfume was like? Was it like that stuff Mamma has on her dressing table?"

"Oh no! It was something much nicer than that, more like flowers." He stared anxiously at Peter.

"Well," said Peter at last. "You wouldn't make that up, I know. I think it *was* Aunt Flossie; it can't be anybody else. It wasn't Mamma, or Maud, or Mrs Edwards, and it doesn't sound like one of the nurses. Yes, I'm sure you're right. I'd know that it was she, even if there hadn't been the part about Uncle Simon Peter."

"Do you really know what to do?" asked Dennis, his eyes brightening. "I've been trying out a few things in the bath myself!"

He told Peter about sailing the ship in the bath, and Peter listened absent-mindedly.

"Yes, that's good," nodded Peter. "We'll have to send them in bottles, though. Look, tomorrow's Friday, so I've got to go to school, but you try and find a good, big bottle that will hold the binoculars. It must be really big, so that it will float even with something large and heavy inside. Any small jam bottle will do for the compass." He thought for a moment. "It doesn't matter what colour the bottles are, but plain glass is best. And they *must* have tight, tight covers."

"But what are we going to do? He could be anywhere! Even if the office knows, they aren't going to tell *us*!" protested Dennis.

Peter stood up and dusted himself off.

"No, we can't get help from anybody else. Don't you see? We must do it all on our own. And they're ours; he gave them to us, so nobody can say anything if we decide–" he did not finish. Mrs Ferguson's voice echoed up the stairs, telling him it was time to go.

Chapter Ten

Friday is pay-day, an important day on every farm. As soon as Mr Ferguson was certain that Annabell was out of danger, he waited only until she had been discharged from hospital, and set off for Virgin Valley. He promised to send Charlie down on the Saturday morning bus to get the latest news of Annabell, and to collect the mare from the paddock out at Barnet Estate where Uncle Edwin had kept her. It was decided too that Peter should come and spend the weekend at Barnet Street, to cheer up his sister and be a help to his mother. Dennis of course would remain there until Annabell was well enough to return home to Virgin Valley.

Peter arrived on Friday afternoon as soon as he could escape from Miss French's, bringing a suitcase full of dirty shirts and pyjamas, and a bottle of paradise plums as a present from Miss French to the invalid.

"This bottle is just right for the compass!" he whispered to Dennis as they helped themselves. "Got anything for the binoculars?"

Dennis nodded, his mouth full. On the pretext of washing and tidying themselves, they went upstairs and Dennis showed Peter his find. He had been very worried about getting a bottle that was large enough, especially as Maud had given him all sorts of jobs to do to make up for missing school. Sighing deeply, he had carried pails upstairs and downstairs for her, fetched brooms, had stood on a chair to get down 'Missis good linen sheet-dem from de top shelf, an' pass four pillow-slip same time, pickney!' Then he was sent to a shop on St. James Street, with a list, a basket, and a pound note pinned inside his shirt, and came back in the hot midday sun with a bottle of syrup, some sugar, tea, flour, saltfish, a bottle of honey, two pounds of brown rice, condensed milk and a dozen eggs. The basket was very heavy, and he had had to stop and rest several times on his way home. It was then that he saw a hardware shop where two men were clearing out rubbish. There, on the sidewalk, covered with thick dust and shavings, lay a huge bottle half-filled with some nasty fluid. The men had said he could take it, and he had washed it out carefully as soon as he got home, and put it in the sun to dry.

"Good," said Peter. "Is Annabell here yet?"

"Upstairs, in the front room," replied Dennis. "I started to tell her, but Mamma wouldn't let me stay long enough to finish."

"Well, never mind that now; we've got a lot to do in the mean time. I'm sure mamma will let us see her later on, or else we'll write her a letter and put it on the tray when Maud takes her supper in."

The two boys then retired to the backyard and Peter carried out a number of careful operations. He approved of the bottle Dennis had found. It was about twelve inches high, very wide, with a strong brass screw-top. Peter produced a small bottle of Cutex nail polish, and proceeded to paint in violent red the legend S.S. FREYA on a large sheet of paper torn from the middle of a drawing book. This he fitted inside the jar, with the lettering on the outside. They were pleased to see that the bright red letters showed up luridly against the whiteness of the paper, and could be read even from upstairs, as they both went up to see. Then he wrote below in smaller letters, 'Property of Pieter Nielsen, Captain of S.S. Freya'. They used a smaller piece of paper for the other bottle with the compass, and Peter used the rest of the nail-polish to paint the threads of each of the caps in turn, before screwing them on as hard as he could while the polish was still wet.

"That'll keep the water out," he explained to Dennis.

"Now what are you going to do?" asked the latter, gazing in pride and some doubt on their handiwork.

"Well, the *Freya* sails in the Caribbean, so we have to send them out into the Caribbean. I've thought it out. Remember Mr Prawl? The one who's a fisherman?' Dennis nodded. "Well, I know him quite well; or, well, Uncle Simon Peter took me to see him more than once, and he always said I could go fishing with him any time I like. So I went round there before school this morning, and asked if he was going out, and if I could go with him. He says he'll take me before day tomorrow morning; I'm to meet him at the pier at four o'clock in the morning, and we'll be back by half-past six at the latest, because he's only taking in fish-pots and he's got to be early for the market."

Dennis looked at his brother with his mouth open.

"O-o-o-oh! You wouldn't *dare*!" breathed Dennis, his eyes wide. "Suppose Mamma and Dad ever found out?" He was struck with awe at the magnitude of the escapade, and terror at what would befall them if they were caught planning anything like this. Peter was even more conscious than Dennis that this was well beyond their ordinary exploits. He was fully prepared for whatever punishment awaited him if he was found out, and, what was more, he intended to protect Dennis completely. He had made up his mind the night before to see this through to the end, and nothing was going to stop him now.

"Don't you worry about that. Nobody's going to find out. But we'll have to borrow Annabell's watch. Mamma's planning to sleep late in the morning, now that Annabell's so much better, and she won't come looking for us until eight o'clock or later." Then a brilliant idea struck him. "Actually, I did leave one of my exercise books up at Miss French's, and I'll need it for my geometry home-work. If I'm late tell them I've gone up there for it. I'll go and pick it up too, when I come back. I can't come strolling in here at a quarter to seven, so I might as well go up there and get it. Fancy Miss French and an exercise book coming in useful!"

Dennis had nothing to do but agree with everything Peter said, and they spent the rest of the afternoon planning ways of making sure they would wake up in time; there was also the matter of getting Peter out of the house unnoticed. In the end they decided to sleep without pillows or blanket, and to put all of their shoes and books under the mattress to make the bed so uncomfortable that proper sleep would be impossible. Peter practised climbing down the verandah at the back, where he could hold on to the ancient honey-suckle creeper that grew there. He was nearly caught at this by Mrs Edwards, bustling out to the kitchen to tell Maud for the tenth time that Miss Annabell was awake and ready for her supper. Fortunately Mrs Edwards did not look up, and was too intent on bothering Maud to hear the faint creaking noises above her head, or to see the unusual quantity of leaves and blossoms floating down from the vine above. But it held, and Peter found just where he should put his feet, and where he should not let all of his weight go on to the trellis that held up the creeper.

After Annabell's supper, Peter and Dennis were allowed to see her for a few minutes.

As soon as they were alone, the three children started the same sentence in one breath:

"Aunt Flossie wants us to–"

They stopped and the boys stared at Annabell as hard as she stared back at them.

"How'd you know?" Annabell sat up and turned to Peter. "I was supposed to tell you."

"Tell me what?" asked Peter, holding back Dennis with one hand.

"To send the binoculars and the compass for Uncle Simon Peter. He's going to need them. We've got to get them out to him. She says it's his last chance to get home. I thought I dreamt it." She turned to Dennis. "It was that afternoon when you came with Dad, and brought the watch for me. I dreamt that she came in. I knew her as soon as I saw her, and she told me that I was going to get better, and come home soon." Her face clouded suddenly. "But we've got to get them to Uncle Simon Peter at once, or he won't come home again. How will we manage it?"

"Well, I saw her too, or else I dreamed the same dream," added Dennis. "It was the same afternoon too. And she said that Peter would know what to do."

"Do you know, Peter?" Annabell's voice sounded unbelieving. "We must do it *quick*, whatever it is! Have you thought of something?"

So the boys told her, as fast as they could, about all of the preparations they had made for dropping the binoculars and compass out at sea next morning.

"That's the only way they might reach him," said Peter. "If somebody had an aeroplane, and could contact the *Freya* by radio, that would be easy. But not even the office could do that, and they wouldn't listen to us if we went to them."

They agreed that that plan was the best, and Annabell giggled just like her usual self when she heard about the books and shoes under the mattress. Just before their mother came upstairs, she undid the watch chain from her neck, and gave it to Peter.

"I'm sorry you have to send away your presents," she said. "but I'd send this too if it would do any good."

"We still have the little *Freya*," said Dennis stoutly. "I only hope there isn't an almighty fuss when Mamma and Dad find out that the other things have disappeared!"

Then the boys were banished from the room, and told to go and have their supper downstairs.

Everything went according to plan. They had stuffed so many things under the coir mattress that it was like sleeping on a sack of stones. Dennis was surprised to find how cold it was without a cover over him. Peter laid out his clothes on a chair by the bed in a special order, so that he could just step into them in the morning. His shoes and the two sealed bottles, safe inside the small bag in which he would carry them, were hidden in the garden where he could find them in the dark next morning. It seemed to Peter that he woke up every ten or fifteen minutes all through that night, but in fact both he and Dennis slept quite soundly on their lumpy bed, waking not more than three or four times. When Peter woke for the last time, the watch was saying twenty minutes to four. It took him what seemed a long time to take this in, then he fell out of bed in a hurry, wondering if he was already too late to catch Mr Prawl. Dennis groaned and turned over. He managed to crawl out of bed and help Peter unlatch the door leading on to the verandah. Peter had to pinch him to wake him sufficiently, as his was the important task of securing the door once Peter was out. Then Dennis suddenly came wide awake, and waited an age in the dark behind the door, straining his ears for any sounds from the direction of the honeysuckle creeper. But there were none, and after testing the bolts again he went back to bed and fell fast asleep.

Peter climbed down the creeper carefully, thanking his stars that he had tried it out on the evening before. Everything looked so different in the dim light. He suddenly wondered if he would meet a policeman on the streets and get arrested. But he had not done anything wrong, and he supposed that other people had to go about at that time of night too. But he went as fast as he could down the street, and along the twisting lanes to the landing used by Mr Prawl and a few other fishermen who supplied the Montego Bay fishmarket.

He was almost out of breath when at last he saw the shabby little white sign at the end of a dark lane. A dim street light showed there, its light shaded on three sides so as not to be visible out at sea. On the fourth side, it shone on the sign which read 'SEPTIMUS PRAWL Boats Tackle Spear-Fishing by Contract.' He pushed the gate into the yard, and went in.

He had never been there alone before, and never by night. The yard stretched down to an untidy jetty, where Mr Prawl's fleet was beached or anchored. This consisted of three old dug-out canoes, a glass bottomed boat for the tourist trade, now used as a store-all, and, anchored by the jetty, the small but serviceable row-boat *Princess Mary* which was Mr Prawl's pride and joy. Two reddish lights were burning down at the jetty, and Peter hurried forward.

"Mr Prawl, it's me! Peter Ferguson!" he called, as Mr Prawl's lanky figure loomed up before him in the dark.

"You almos' late. Come on this way, boy, an' don' interfere with anything!"

Peter got aboard somehow in the dark, his shoes in one hand and the bag in the other. He was thankful that it was too dark for Mr Prawl to notice the bag and ask awkward questions. In another minute they had unshipped their oars, cast off, and were pulling steadily out towards the middle of the bay. It was still, with few stars. The air felt cold and damp, and Mr Prawl said it might rain before morning. Peter tried to make out where they were going, but in the obscurity he could make no sense of their movements, and neither Mr Prawl nor the man who was his sole assistant, were very communicative. At first Peter thought they must be going to the Bogue Islands, but then they changed course several times, finally making towards the other side of the harbour near to the hospital. As they approached the mouth of the harbour they rowed faster, and Mr Prawl, whose pipe was forever going out and having to be re-lit, complained and swore at the carelessness of the people on shore who had let lights burn where they could be seen out at sea. Like Mr Evans of Cedar Hill, Mr Prawl was holding himself ready for the invasion. His assistant, apparently named Mento, paid no attention to any of this, as he was in any case doing most of the work. It took them a long time to clear the harbour, or so it seemed to Peter, listening to the regular glop-ploonge, glop-ploonge of the oars as the waves smacked against the boat.

When they left the harbour Peter was aware of a change in the motion of the boat. The waves felt larger, too, and the boat started a steady sideways rocking as though they were going against a current. The air smelled different too, fresher and saltier. Peter had decided that he would wait until they had pulled up the last fish-pot, and then drop his bottles over the side while Mr Prawl and Mento were busy. He knew that if they ever suspected what he was going to do, he would never have a chance of carrying out his plan, and a report would be lodged at Barnet Street before the day was over.

But in spite of that, he could not help enjoying himself. The novelty of the boat ride over the dark sea, the sounds and smells of it, and the very real risk made him wide awake and eerily happy. He felt he understood Uncle Simon Peter better than ever before; this life between sea and sky was the only life worth living. He decided that he would be a sailor when he grew up, and travel all over the world as Uncle Simon

Peter did.

After about an hour's steady rowing, the boat slowed down and Peter, instructed by Mr Prawl, was able to make out something small and steady in the dimness ahead of the boat. It was the marker for the first fish-pot, a glass float with a phosphorescent core. In a few swift strokes Mento brought the boat close to it, and then they hauled it in. Peter was given the shaded hurricane lantern to hold, and Mr Prawl and Mento emptied the long basket into a big tub in the middle of the boat. There was evidently not as much in it as Mr Prawl expected, for the grumbling started again, louder this time.

'How many more fish-pots are you going to empty?" asked Peter, hoping to cheer up Mr Prawl.

"Six-seven more, maybe, but I don' like the breeze this morning! It's a land-breeze, which is a funny thing right now. Not suppose to have a breeze like that, this time of night, this time of year. Bad weather round the area, nearby. Could get rough, an' Prawl is a man don't stay out in bad weather. What you think, Mento?" The two men went off into a long, muttered discussion of the possible significance of the weather, and ignored Peter completely.

By the time they got to the third fish-pot, a faint greyness was beginning to cast its twilight over everything. The tub was quarter full of fish, and the waves slower but heavier. Even Peter could see that. Mr Prawl's pipe had gone out altogether.

"The next one is the furthest out," he said to Peter, suddenly remembering his existence. "Turn down the wick an' blow out the lantern for me. Good. Well, I was thinkin' we should turn back now, but we don' get much, and that one is always the best one. This weather goin' to stop anybody from goin' out tomorrow or Monday."

Peter gripped the handle of his bag and prepared to watch for the best moment. In the event, he had no trouble at all. A fine drizzle started, and they had enough trouble finding the little buoy without paying much notice to him. He got the bottles out, suddenly wondering whether the bright red paint would show up in the dimness. The fish-pot, when it was emptied, turned out to be the best indeed, and the tub was almost full of wriggling, jumping fish as Mento threw the basket back into the water and released the lines that held the float. Mr Prawl, sucking on an empty pipe and cursing the rain, pulled steadily away from the buoy, and Peter let the two bottles slide into the water. Both men pulled hard on the oars and the boat turned away from the float in a long curve. Peter looked back and saw two whitish things bobbing on the water near the float, but at that distance even he could hardly have told what they were.

Getting back into the harbour turned out to be quite a struggle, and Peter soon found out why Mr Prawl had been worried about a land breeze. Even though they did not depend on a sail, which would have been useless, the boat made way with difficulty. There seemed to be waves coming in all directions, and the boat showed a strong inclination to go either west to Lucea or east to Falmouth, or even back out to sea, but not into Montego Bay harbour. The fine drizzle turned into a misty rain, so that you could see nothing clearly. The coastline disappeared behind a wall of smoky cloud, and Mr Prawl's curses turned on the harbourmaster, the war, and the shape of the bay, which made Peter wonder anxiously if they would ever get to land again. But at last the familiar dockhouses came into view in the thin light, and about fifteen minutes later Peter was stepping off on to the tumbledown jetty, and thanking Mr Prawl from the bottom of his heart.

"A pleasure, a pleasure, young fellow. Just let me know when you care to come. Always welcome anybody from the Captain. Here, Mento, string up some fish and send for Captain. Tell him I hope to see him any time he can spare a little time; just let me know an' I'll come round to the house. Well, goodbye young fellow, an' remember me to the family!"

With that a heavy string of green parrot fish, with a large snapper and two small goat fish was thrust into his hands by Mento. Peter set off as fast as his stiff legs would carry him, wondering what on earth to do with the fish, and how to explain them to his mother?

A clock struck seven as he crossed St. James Street. Very few people were up, and the rain was getting heavier. He left the fish hidden in the hedge at Miss French's, and was let in through the back door by Hermine, the cook, who seemed quite unsurprised to see him. He explained hurriedly about the forgotten book, grabbed up his raincoat as well, and left before Miss French had time to find out he was there. On the way to Barnet Street he decided to tell his mother that the fish was a gift from Mr Prawl, whom he had met that morning. This was certainly true, but not in the way she would understand it.

Peter was at Barnet Street by half past seven. He whistled in the street to let Dennis know that he was back. He was beginning to wonder whether the little fool had overslept, and how he would brazen it out with Maud and the Edwards, when an answering whistle came from upstairs, and he saw Dennis waving to him from the upstairs verandah. A moment later Dennis had opened the side door into the garden and was beckoning him in.

"Did it o.k.?" Dennis whispered eagerly. "Gosh! What you're going to do with all that fish? Maud's in the kitchen. You'd better give it to her. What made you go and bring that back for?"

But Maud, and later Mrs Ferguson, accepted Peter's story of the fish, and the missing book, and even went so far as to praise him for going out early, and on a rainy morning, and getting such a handsome present. They had the fish for lunch, and it was very good indeed.

Chapter Eleven

The children spent the rest of the weekend very quietly. The boys slept late on Sunday, and went to night service with Maud at the Parish Church. Annabell seemed to tire very easily, and slept most of the day. Now and then in the days that followed, Peter worried about what they had done, and sometimes he missed his binoculars very badly. The children agreed not to talk about them: they had done the only thing they felt was right, even though it was crazy, and had cost them two of their most precious possessions. Annabell wanted to give Peter the watch to take back to Miss French's, but he said it was a lady's watch, and should be kept by Annabell herself. So she slept with it under her pillow.

During the week that followed, Annabell got better rapidly, and Mrs Ferguson began to talk of taking her home soon. Annabell would do better at Virgin Valley, away from the noise and dust of Montego Bay. Also,

Maud was not in the best of tempers, having been tried sorely by Mrs Edwards, and Annabell too had taken the worthy lady in dislike. Trying to be kind, Mrs Edwards was always telling Annabell gruesome stories about the war, or recounting the details of Aunt Flossie's last illness and funeral, and what she had said and done on all these memorable occasions. Mrs Ferguson managed to put a stop to most of it, but there had been the day when Mrs Edwards asserted that German submarines were sailing right around Jamaica day and night on the look-out for ships, and even coming into port when they felt like it. She had brought in *The Daily Gleaner* of March 4, to read out some nonsensical story about a 'mysterious craft' seen off Dry Harbour by three fishermen. Annabell had begged to be taken home the next day, and after that she pretended to be asleep whenever Mrs Edwards entered the room. Then Dennis, at first good as gold, had taken up Annabell's cause against Mrs Edwards, and had put a dead lizard in the Edwards's bed. At least, she was sure that Dennis knew something about that lizard, for he had been quite bored and unconcerned when Mrs Edwards rushed in screaming. It was time they went home.

So on the Friday of that week, Maud and Dennis were packed off on the bus to Somerton to get everything ready for Annabell's return, and to tell Mr Ferguson that Uncle Edwin would again borrow the estate van to bring Mrs Ferguson and Annabell home on Sunday. Fuel rationing was strict, but he would be able to manage somehow.

In the days that followed Annabell's return to Virgin Valley, she improved even faster than she had at Barnet Street. She and Dennis took their codliver oil quietly, instead of spitting it out in the garden or giving it to the dogs. Nobody had any nightmares, and the lamp was no longer left burning in the passage at night. The weather turned dry and bright, with starlight so clear that the children could go to bed without candle or lamp.

"Don't you think it's time for Uncle Simon Peter to come back again?" asked Dennis one evening at supper.

"We can't tell nowadays, dear," replied Mrs Ferguson. "Perhaps a letter will come soon. Everything is so difficult now! I hear that some people who wanted to go to England to volunteer for war work, had to go to Panama of all places, and wait over three weeks for a passage to England! I'm sure we'll hear from him soon." Dennis looked dissatisfied, and Annabell had to kick him under the table in case he let out the story of the compass and the binoculars.

A few days later, on Saturday the 14th of March, a day which none of them ever forgot, Annabell saw her mother hastily cutting something out of the lower right hand corner of *The Daily Gleaner*. Then she disappeared upstairs for a long time, and came down with her eyes very red and her nose swollen. Neither Annabell nor Dennis read much in the newspapers beyond the headlines (sometimes), the titles of the movies showing in Kingston and Montego Bay, and the adventures of the Gump family. They therefore did not miss a small clipping from the front page, and thought nothing of its disappearance. Annabell did think it odd of her mother to go off to her bedroom like that in the middle of a busy Saturday, but Peter was expected home any minute, and she and Dennis were on the look-out for every vehicle that went by on the main road below the hill. They had to wait until dusk, for he came up on the last market truck and stood the whole way.

During supper Peter whispered to Annabell and

Dennis that he had news of a very important kind to pass on to them. As soon as they were able, they went off and held a whispered conference in the boys' room.

"What's the matter? What's happened to you?" asked Annabell, seeing a frown gather on Peter's face. "Don't tell me somebody's found out!"

Dennis gasped.

"No, no, no! Not that at all. Much worse." Peter was going through his pockets carefully, as though searching for something stowed away with especial care. "Has our *Gleaner* come yet? I'll have to show this to Mamma and Dad too."

"Oh it came long ago!" burst in Dennis. "Mr Jones brought it over early for Dad. I saw him come up with it from morning!"

"Why? What's the *Gleaner* got to do with us?" asked Annabell, her voice cracking a little. "I looked at it after Mamma did, and all I noticed was that Mamma had cut out something from the front page, down at the bottom."

She felt very cold all of a sudden, and shivered.

Peter at last pulled out a small scrap of paper, carefully folded in two and tucked in an envelope. He spread it out in the light of the candle.

"Well, read that and you'll see why she cut it out of our paper! She doesn't want us to know!"

They all bent over the scrap of the paper, peering at it in the pale light of the candle. The print was fine and hard to read. At first Dennis thought that the other two were just acting grown-up and mysterious to show off; then he heard Annabell draw her breath sharply. He forced himself to read the tiny print until Peter came to his rescue and read it out aloud.

"Another tanker sunk by enemy in the Caribbean,"

read Peter. "Washington, March 13. The United States Navy Department has announced the sinking of a tanker by enemy submarine in the Caribbean area. Four survivors described how the U-boat ran down two of the lifeboats on the rocks. Some of the survivors drifted for a week. Thirty members of the tanker's crew are missing.

"The Navy announced today that six survivors from a Norwegian ship sunk by submarines had arrived at an east coast port aboard another vessel. The survivors consisted of the Captain of the ship and five members of his crew. The Captain said his vessel was sunk by shellfire after battle with two submarines. The ship's single gun was disabled, but the crew almost mutinied when ordered to take to the boats. The men hoped to repair the gun and continue the fight.

"The Navy tonight announced the torpedoing of two merchant ships off the Atlantic coast. One described as 'small United States merchant ship' was torpedoed in the Caribbean area and the other as a 'small Norwegian merchant ship' torpedoed off the Atlantic coast."

That was all.

"Maybe it's not the *Freya*," mumbled Peter, not looking at the others. "No names. They can't put names in. But I thought I'd better cut this out and keep it."

They stood silent in the flickering light a long time. No one wanted to say anything, or to have to be the first to break that silence. Dennis looked at Peter's face, frowning harshly in the dimness. It must be Uncle Simon Peter, then; Peter would not look like that if it wasn't true. A cold tightness gathered in his chest. Annabell was staring at Peter too, with feverish, overbright eyes. Suddenly she snatched the paper from Peter and thrust one edge of it into the flame of the candle.

"Let's do the ceremony again! Right *now*!" she cried as the paper burned to ash.

"What's the use? It's too late!" exclaimed Dennis, his face pale.

"Don't say that!" Annabell winced as if she had been stung. "There's always use! Get the ship and we'll do it now!"

She was so insistent that they gave way. They all washed hurriedly and set up the tent in Annabell's room. There were no peenies this time, so Peter stuck the stump of candle in his tooth-glass and read by that light. Then they went to bed. A week later Mrs Ferguson told Annabell and Dennis that Uncle Simon Peter might be in trouble, they must all be brave. Another week went by; no letter or telegram came. Mr Ferguson inquired of the *Freya* in Montego Bay, to no avail. It was the end of March. Uncle Simon Peter had not been heard from for over four months. Mrs Ferguson gave up hope and cried herself to sleep at nights. Her mood communicated itself to Maud, who got fretful and complained of her age and the wickedness of the times, the work of the Devil.

But in April Annabell got stronger and stronger, as though she had never been ill, as if she had not a care in the world. Dennis and Peter, too, seemed very well and growing fast all of a sudden. Peter's uniforms were tight across his shoulders, and both boys had to have new shoes, even though their old shoes were hardly worn out yet. Annabell resumed her evening classes with Miss Webster, and announced that she was going to work very hard and get to go to school in Montego Bay like Peter. They asked no more questions about Uncle Simon Peter, and their mother was glad that they knew nothing about the clipping hidden away in a drawer of the bureau in her room.

Then one day, when the Easter holidays were nearly over, she was going through the mending with Annabell in her bedroom upstairs and lamenting the loss of buttons on Peter's clothes. At the same instant they both heard the sound of a car engine on the drive.

"Uncle Simon Peter!" shrieked Annabell, and tore down the steps two at a time. She had not looked out of the window to see who it was. Mrs Ferguson heard her yelling to Peter and Dennis to 'Come! Come quick!' She went over to the window, feeling quite sick, and wondering who on earth it could be. But when she looked out, she stood still for a long moment. She could see down the length of the drive as it curved down the hill, and there was the little black Austin toiling up the slope, her three children standing on the fenders on either side. It seemed years before she could tear her gaze away and run to the head of the stairs.

Maud was on the verandah, her apron over her head, her glasses on the floor, weeping and rocking her body as if she were demented. Leebert had left the pump and was running down the interval shouting "Missa Joe! Missa Joe! Captain come! Captain come!" The two dogs were running alongside the car, barking their heads off. Everyone seemed to have gone utterly mad.

It was a long, long time before the house was quiet that evening. Even supper was served in strange bits and pieces, because they were all too excited to sit in one place for long, and Uncle Simon Peter had to be everywhere, with everyone, all of the time. He would not stay still, though they noticed that he moved with less than his usual vigour. His beard had been trimmed very close, and under his tan he seemed paler. But he

laughed as much as ever, with an arm around first Maud, and then Mrs Ferguson, as they struggled to open the tin of American ham he had brought, fry pancakes, and slice bread.

After supper they shared a bottle of red wine in the living room; the children thought it quite nasty, but would never have dreamed of refusing the privilege of tasting a grown-up drink. Uncle Simon Peter drank very little, and when Dennis climbed up in his lap, his face twitched with pain.

"Oh, but you are too big at last for this, Dennis! An old man I am now, and it is in your lap that I should be sitting!" he exclaimed. The others laughed and the incident was forgotten. There was so much he wanted to know: how was Peter doing at school (he made him put on his blazer so he could see how he looked), was he on the football team, did he like the new subjects, geometry, algebra, and foreign languages, and did he ever get down to the sea. At this point it seemed to the three children that Uncle Simon Peter glanced at Peter in a very odd way. Then he changed the subject abruptly, and said that he was temporarily in charge of another ship, the *Margery Daw*.

"Herr Hitler did not like the old *Freya*, or me. We were sunk, but I am not supposed to tell you when or where. What difference that would make now, I cannot think. But it is very bad; several ships of Norway have been lost this spring, and many of the officers and men I have known for years. Of my own crew only five others came to land." His eyes seemed fixed on a remote scene visible only to himself. "I do not want to got to sea any more, but a man must do what is needed, no matter how he feels. There is some reason why we were spared, the six of us. That I know."

Then he shook off the strange mood, and began to ask questions about the farm, and whether the rationing of gas had hit them very hard. The three children sat quietly in the shadows of the living room and let the conversation flow around them unnoticed. Annabell's attention was taken up by Uncle Simon Peter's left hand, that seemed to shake, very slighty, and uncontrollably, chiefly when he was trying to keep it still. Then he would hold it in his right hand for a little while until the trembling stopped; but presently it would start to shake again, and he would have to grasp it with his other hand once more. His left leg was inclined to shake too, with an odd life of its own. Dennis kept thinking, 'He's got smaller! Why, he's much smaller than I thought! How could I have believed he was so big? He's still much bigger than Dad, but he used to be bigger than an elephant!' Peter saw none of this. He only saw that Uncle Simon Peter's eyes, deep and bright as ever, now gleamed with a steady, sombre light that he had never seen before in anyone's expression. There was something distant about that look, and yet it was not sad, or angry, or cold, or anything like that. Peter kept trying to feel his way into this new expression in Uncle Simon Peter's eyes; there was something that he felt he ought to understand, but could not quite grasp. 'Perhaps he's tired,' he thought, but he knew that that was not the answer. Then he thought, 'The sea-battle, of course, they had only the one gun against two submarines, and all those men were his friends. It's worse than being torpedoed! I wonder why the subs didn't just torpedo them and leave?' But that was not the whole truth either. 'Of course he wants to stay here, now. He's so used to the *Freya* that he won't be happy in any other ship. She was more like home than anything else!' And even as he thought that, he knew that that was only another small part of the truth. With a strange surging in his heart he wondered what Uncle Simon Peter would say if and when he heard of the fate of the binoculars and the compass. He had already planned to saythat they were at Miss French's, for none of them had the courage to face him with the truth.

The next day Uncle Simon Peter stayed in bed late, a most unusual happening. After his breakfast, he went for a slow walk down the hill with Annabell and Dennis, and heard how Annabell had actually been in hospital for five days (she was now quite proud of this for some reason), and how Benjie had treed Peter in the Christmas holidays, and had had to be put in the small back pasture. Then Annabell confessed that she wanted to go to school in Montego Bay, like Peter, and Dennis became silent and disconsolate. Uncle Simon Peter began to cheer Dennis by saying something about all of them living with him at Barnet Street, when they turned around at the bottom of the drive to walk back to the house. As they turned around Dennis exclaimed,

"Look! Annabell look! The lady on the verandah! She's waving to us! It's Aunt Flossie again!"

Annabell looked up in time to see a tall lady in a dress of deep blue move along the verandah of the house above them. As she vanished through the door opening into the living room, she seemed to blow a kiss to them. It was all over in a few seconds. Annabell blinked.

"What are you saying, Dennis?" asked Uncle Simon Peter, who had not been looking in the direction of the house. "What are you talking about? Aunt Flossie? Where? What do you mean?"

"I – I'm not sure," stammered Dennis. He went brick red, then pale, and then red again. "I thought I saw a lady in a blue dress, waving to us from up on the verandah."

"You're not trying to make game of an old man, eh?" Uncle Simon Peter stared first at him, then at the house, his breath suddenly coming hard. "I see no lady anywhere! This is nonsense, boy!"

He looked so terrible that Annabell hastened to rescue the wretched Dennis.

"It's just that we've been talking about Aunt Flossie a lot these days," she said quickly, "because Dennis doesn't really remember her, and Maud tells us lots of things. It's Mamma or Maud whom you saw, Dennis."

But they both knew that Mrs Ferguson was down in Somerton visiting friends, and Maud would not be on the verandah waving to anyone at any time. They went back to the house in silence.

Chapter Twelve

In the afternoon Uncle Simon Peter sat on the verandah with Mrs Ferguson and the children. Annabell was helping her mother with an embroidered tablecloth, though her task consisted solely of matching and sorting various embroidery silks. She had a fine eye for colour, but the skill of a cobbler in sewing, a fact much lamented by her mother. As he watched Annabell bending over the pile of multicoloured skeins, Uncle Simon Peter shook his head and sighed.

"It is strange you can do that so well, Annabell, and none of us would be much good at it. Yust as sometimes a man does a task he knows is impossible, and later on when it is all over and done, he doesn't know how he did it."

He took up his pipe, but his left hand shook so much that Mrs Ferguson told Peter in a sharp voice to strike a match for his uncle. When the pipe was lit, Uncle Simon Peter stretched out his long legs and gazed at the cane-fields below the house and the dark green hills beyond.

"I did not expect ever to see you again," he said in a soft voice that only Annabell heard.

"Did you say something, Uncle Simon Peter?" asked Mrs Ferguson, turning her head towards him. She was busy tracing a complicated pattern of orchids and their leaves on to squares of bleached linen. Her mouth was full of pins, and there was an absent-minded look in her eyes.

"I was thinking of how we came to land," he said, rousing himself. "Yust six of us alone escaped from the *Freya*, in the end, and I did not expect us to make our way to land, or even to be picked up. We knew always that submarines were near us, for many reports came in from other ships, some of which they have sunk. Several ships of Norway among them, and men whom I have known these thirty years. But that is not strange in war. No, that is not what I was thinking about."

Peter looked up and caught Annabell's eye. All three children went very still.

"Peggy, I have not told you any of this, because I do not understand it myself. None of the six of us who came ashore can understand it. You see, we were coming through bad weather, for several days, rain and a heavy sea that kept us back. Sometimes the radio was too bad for us to hear any message, but one night – our last night on the *Freya* – we were warned of submarines ahead in the area to which we must go. By dawn next day the weather had cleared, and we heard a distress call from another ship, quite near she was, that had just been torpedoed. They are taking to the lifeboats, so we change course to meet them, and wonder if we will meet the submarine first. I must not tell you where, but when we search for them we find no boats at all, only small wreckage. That is all. We move on, and we do not know where the submarine has gone, but the men begin to be angry. That ship was a small merchant ship of Norway, and her crew armed with nothing but small arms, while on the *Freya* we have a gun to defend ourselves.

"The day continued clear and bright. We were making good speed, and could be in port in two more days if all goes well. But all does not go well. At noon a submarine was sighted, surfaced a mile or two away, and then another beside the first. Perhaps they met because of enyine troubles, I do not know, for they do not seem to have been following us, and they did not approach to torpedo at once, as I expected. Bjornsen was master-gunner, and knew his yob well. They shelled us, you see, and we held them off for a short while. But two against one, with a single gun, is hopeless. Bjornsen was killed and the gun broken from its moorings. Both the enyine room and the bridge were hit, and I knew the *Freya* was lost. But old Nansen the mate wanted to try and repair the damage, and keep on fighting. The others were yust as bad. They could not do any repair in less than an hour, and before that hour is over, the *Freya* would be long since at the bottom of the sea."

He sighed and shook his head.

"But in the end they all had to obey me. We got our two life-boats in the water, and those still alive went into them. Then one of the submarines came close, even though they could see we had abandoned ship. They did not like the *Freya*, I suppose. She was already sinking but they blew her up while we were still close to her side. The other boat went down with her, and then they left us alone. The clouds gathered as afternoon went on. Everyone in the boat had some kind of wound, and I myself–" he touched the right side of his head, "I got the last blow of all, as the explosion threw the wreckage all around us. But it did not bleed much, and I had more to think of than a sore head.

"We had nothing to steer by, not even a pocket compass, you see. We knew where we were, but there the currents are strange, and more likely to take you across the Atlantic to Africa or round and round in circles. Then the weather grew worse, with a heavy swell and rain at night, though little wind. By midnight we could not tell whether we were north, south, east, or west of where the *Freya* went down, and no idea where land might be. But I made a kind of sail, and I said to myself, 'We will go north. We will meet the convoy. It is very simple.' I said nothing to the others, for to myself it was all very clear. Where is north? I shut my eyes, and in my mind saw the sky above the clouds, full of stars. In the black night I shut my eyes and took our bearings, a crazy thing to do. Never once did I ask myself, nor did the other men say, what nonsense is this that I am doing? Then before dawn, in the grey, dim rain, I looked and saw a ship far ahead of us. She could easily have missed us, but I knew she would not. And yet it was an hour later at least before we were safely on board her. When we were in port and the doctors busy with my head, Nansen came to me in the hospital. He scratched his beard and said that we seem to have been very lucky, did I know the *Thomas Yefferson* was close to us when I rigged the sail? "A current must have carried us," I said. "None that I know of," he answered, "but I am very grateful, whatever it was." And he went away.

Mrs Ferguson picked up her forgotten embroidery and smiled at Uncle Simon Peter. "It was meant to be so," she said simply. "None of us will ever understand. We can only be grateful, like Mr Nansen. Where is he now, Uncle Simon Peter? Where are the others who escaped with you?"

"Most of them are in the American Navy, for there is no new Norwegian ship in which we might go." He pulled hard on his pipe, and a twinkle came to his eyes. "Nansen has a shore yob in Washington, so that he can visit the naval hospital, he says. But I think he is visiting one of the nurses, and not the hospital!"

Mrs Ferguson laughed and took a skein of pale lavender silk from the bundle in Annabell's hands.

"But when I try to remember that night, and what I did, my head aches. Fifty-four years in all I have been at sea, and never have I done such a thing, or even heard of it." He rose stiffly from the chair. "Flossie would say I am too old for all this. Perhaps she is right. Perhaps she is right."

He was silent after that, and did not join in the conversation as Mrs Ferguson asked Peter about his games equipment; the books he would need for the coming term, and whether he would be allowed to keep a tin of Ovaltine at Miss French's.

As soon as the children we alone, Dennis burst out,

"Why don't we tell him?" Don't you think we should tell him? *I* think he ought to know!" he looked hard at Peter and Annabell, his legs apart and his chest stuck out.

Annabell was biting her fingernails, a habit she fell into in rare moments of perplexity. She stole a glance at Peter, but she said nothing. Peter looked unhappy.

"How can we tell him? It won't make sense to anybody! In fact, it looks worse now, to send them off like that, when he lost his own things in the *Freya*. I don't know what I'll say if he asks for them back!"

Dennis turned pale.

"And anyway he's feeling too awful now," said Annabell. "Can't you see that, Dennis? D'you want him to feel even worse than he does, stupid?"

"But – but –" began Dennis.

"I think Annabell's right, Dennis." Peter's voice was strange and hoarse; it cracked in queer ways. "Not yet. It's not fair; not yet."

So that was where it was left, and all that the children did was to have another ceremony, at Annabell's insistence, for saying thanks. Uncle Simon Peter did not mention the subject again, and the matter was closed. He went back to Montego Bay the following day, and then two days after, to their surprise, the Austin appeared once more, driven by Uncle Edwin this time, with Uncle Simon Peter grinning beside him. There was little enough to grin about when they heard his news; he had been sent on sick-leave for two months, and the *Margery Daw* had sailed with the first officer in charge.

"Now at last I well spend *my* birthday here!" He sat down heavily in his favourite chair on the verandah, and laughed at Dennis labouring over his arithmetic homework in a corner.

"How old will you be, Uncle Simon Peter?" asked Dennis before his mother could stop him.

"Of full years I'll be as a man should be," was all the answer he got. "If you look in the Bible you will see the number." He laughed again, the deep, rumbling laugh they knew so well. "The good Maud alone is ahead of me by one year. But no doubt you think us too old for you, Sir Parrot!"

Once more the spare room smelled of bayrum and Yardleys shaving soap, and Uncle Simon Peter taught Dennis and Annabell several new card-games, helped them with their home-work, and began to give Annabell lessons in Norwegian, for fun. She learned about krone and centner, and how to work out what they were in English money and weight, and he taught her how to say "I love you" in Norwegian, because every girl should know that. The only pity was that the holidays were over, and Peter was not there. He came home for the weekend of April 25, and Uncle Simon Peter insisted on taking them all to the beach. Mrs Ferguson tried to get him to rest, but he only laughed and asked what did she think he was doing? He rode round the farm with Mr Ferguson, went with Annabell and Dennis to watch the drilling on the common, and became so popular in the district that he very soon had more invitations than he could manage, and Mr Ferguson had to pass the word quietly that he was on sick-leave, and was to rest by doctor's orders.

Peter and Uncle Edwin came up from Montego Bay for Uncle Simon Peter's birthday. It was actually May the 1st, but as that was a Friday, an impossible day for Uncle Edwin, the celebration was put off for Saturday the 2nd. Mrs Ferguson and Maud came as close to a quarrel as they ever did in their lives as to who should do the cooking. Maud had a Rhode Island rooster rearing for a special occasion, and sniffed when she heard that the Somerton butcher had promised Mrs Ferguson a rib roast of surpassing excellence. Then there was the problem of the birthday cake; should it be Mrs Ferguson's legendary chocolate cake, or Maud's fruitcake from a recipe of Aunt Flossie's, with the soft, creamy icing that melted in your mouth? In the end they reached a compromise: the rooster was allowed to wander at large unaware of his escape from the axe, and Maud made her fruitcake in silent triumph. Uncle Edwin produced a box of blue birthday cake candles, which were arranged on the cake in the figures '70'. Mr Ferguson brought out a bottle of old Cuban rum which Uncle Edwin swore had been given to Grandpa as a present, and the children went down to Miss Ida's shop for tissue paper to wrap their presents. These had given them much thought and worry, especially as they had had so little time to get them ready. Peter plucked up his courage and asked the advice of his form master. With the help of Mr Miller, he found and framed a print of an eighteenth century map of the West Indies, taken from the moth-eaten remnants of a nineteenth century geography text. Annabell bought him three handkerchiefs, and helped by her mother, embroidered on each of them the initials 'P.N.' The letters were rather wobbly, but they were the best she ever did in her life. Dennis considered hard and long, and then had to borrow half of Annabell's pocketmoney, as well as a shilling from his mother, in order to buy Uncle Simon Peter a tiny mouth-organ at Miss Ida's, left over from the Christmas stock. He had been admiring it for months, in fact.

The party went off very well, especially the toast from the oldest present, given by Maud.

"Twenty an' t'ree years now Captain an' me is beknownst to one anedda,' she pronounced, her glass of wine clutched in her hand. "An' all dat time 'im is a gentleman, h'especially where it concern my Missis. She always tell me, 'Maud, de Captain an' I will never part. 'Im will always come 'ome safe an' sound, no matter where 'im travel. See 'ow she talk truth? Ef you young pickney can come wid quarter de sense what Captain 'ave, maybe you will not too stupid after all. 'Ealth, 'appiness, an' God blessin' on Captain!" And she raised her glass for the toast.

They sat on the verandah very late that night, talking of all sorts of things. Uncle Simon Peter told them how he first met Mr Prawl, who had not been above emptying other people's fish-pots out of spite. But a fight in a bar cured him of that; Uncle Simon Peter had had to throw the other man into the street, and drag Mr Prawl into a back room until the commotion was over. Mr Prawl received fourteen stitches in his face and arms at the hospital.

"But a stitch in time saves nine," chuckled Uncle Simon Peter. "It taught him a good lesson."

Then he told them stories of fights at sea between fishermen and the sharks that followed the boats hoping for offal. Once again he told the story of how he came to be captain of the *Freya*, just after the Great War when shipping was in chaos. Finally, to please Dennis and Annabell, he sang a song in Norwegian. Then they had prayers and went to bed.

The next morning was Sunday, and the whole family went off to church save for Uncle Edwin who had to return to Montego Bay, and Uncle Simon Peter who was persuaded by Mrs Ferguson to stay in bed. The service seemed rather dull that day, and the children were just nodding off during the sermon when there was a small stir at the back of the church. One of the elderly women sitting near the back door came to the bench where the Fergusons were seated, and whispered in Mr Ferguson's ear. He looked around quickly. Charlie was out in the church yard looking anxiously inside. Mr Ferguson went out and spoke to him, and then signalled to his wife and children to follow him.

"Uncle Simon Peter is ill," he said. "We must hurry. Charlie's riding on to Adelphi for the doctor. Come now, everybody in."

The drive back seemed to take forever, Mrs Ferguson sat with her hands clasped tightly in her lap, and Mr Ferguson gave all his attention to Jenny and the pot holes in the road At the foot of the drive the children were turned out to lighten the buggy. They could see Maud standing on the verandah looking out for them. The buggy reached the house before they did, and when they arrived they were told to stay outside and keep quiet. And there they stayed, quite forgotten, while the hours went by, the doctor came, and Maud and their mother hurried to and fro. At about three o'clock Mrs Ferguson remembered that no one had had anything to eat since breakfast time. She sent Annabell and Peter to the pantry to make cheese sandwiches and mix lemonade. She herself had nothing, but Mr Ferguson ate one of the sandwiches and had a cup of coffee which Annabell made for him.

At five o'clock Uncle Edwin returned, summoned by a message taken by a passing truck-driver. The doctor had left, saying he should be called again if there was any change. The children saw their parents' faces as they accompanied the doctor to his car. They did not have to ask any questions.

"I want to see him to say goodbye," said Annabell to Peter, as they sat on the verandah, trying to make themselves as small as possible.

"Me too," said Dennis, though he was terrified of the room upstairs, and all the hushed comings and goings.

"I think he's asleep," said Peter. "We'll have to ask Mamma."

Nobody relished the idea of doing that. They sat and pondered this for a while. Dad had left the house with Uncle Edwin to carry out a few belated chores on the farm. Mamma had gone to lie down for a few minutes' rest. The coast was clear. With one look at each other, they got up and went softly upstairs. The door to the spare room was slightly ajar, and their bare feet made no sound as they tip-toed in.

The gold light of sunset hung level in the room, and Annabell could hear flocks of birds on their way home gossipping and quarrelling outside. Uncle Simon Peter was lying on his back, very still, with his hands on the coverlet and his eyes half-open. There was a peculiar look to one side of his face, as if it had gone slack. For a dreadful moment Dennis thought that he was dead already. Then the right side of his face moved in a faint smile that widened into a lop-sided grin, and the eye above twinkled. His right hand stirred a little, as if beckoning to them, and Dennis immediately forgot everything but that this was Uncle Simon Peter, whom he could never be frightened of, no matter what. They went quietly up to the bed.

Annabell leaned over the pillow and kissed his cheek, smoothing down the bristly whiskers with her fingers.

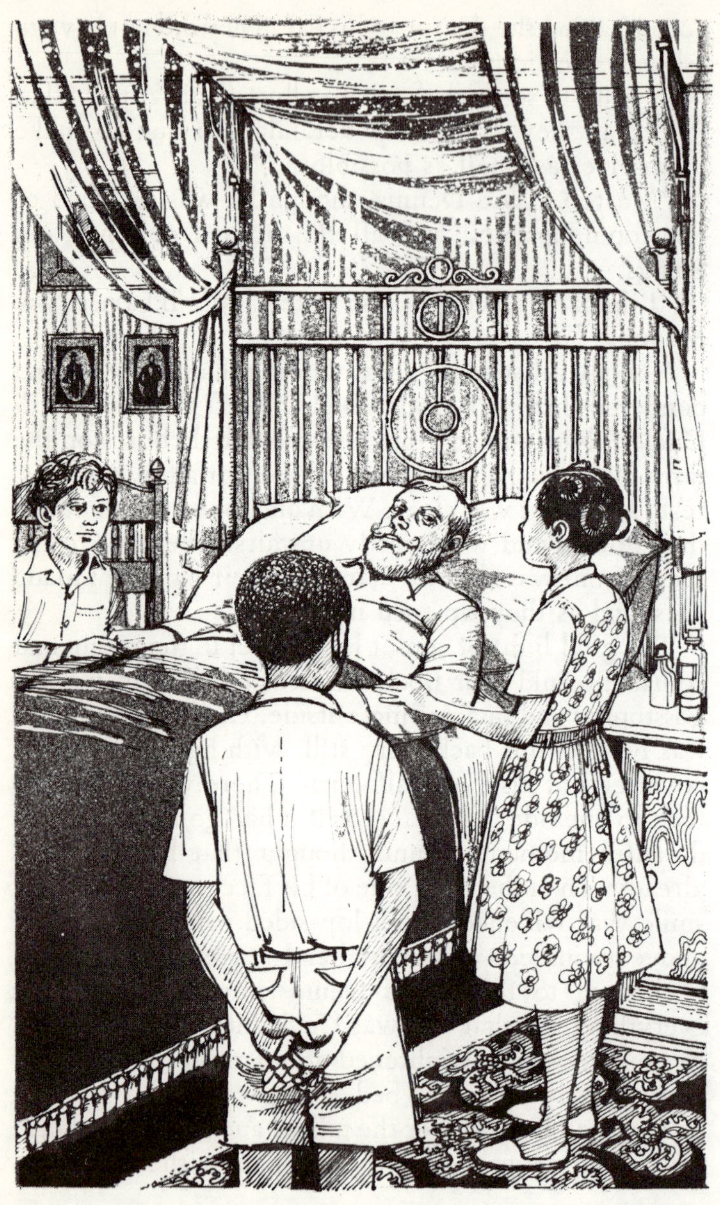

Peter found himself standing behind Annabell, smiling down at him as if they two shared a secret joke, the best in the world. Uncle Simon Peter reached out feebly and took Dennis's hand. He looked at them brightly with his one sound eye, the smile playing mischeviously on his face as they watched. The evening wind lifted the long white muslin curtains and flapped them across the bed. Then his lips seemed to move on one side, and Annabell bent closer to catch the words.

To Peter it sounded like 'yea-elskeh-day, yea-elskeh-day'. To Annabell it was quite clear: 'Jeg elske daeg. Jeg elske daeg.' In Norwegian, I love you, I love you.

Suddenly Peter and Dennis heard the sound together. It was a small, high voice:

"Blow the wind southerly, southerly, southerly,
Blow merry breeze, o'er the bonny blue sea.
Blow the wind southerly, southerly, southerly,
Blow bonny breeze, my true love to me.

They told me last night there were ships in the offing
And I went me down to the deep rolling sea;
But ne'er did I see it, where ever it be,
The barque that is bearing my true love to me.

So blow the wind southerly, southerly, southerly,
Blow the wind south o'er the deep rolling sea;
Blow the wind southerly, southerly, southerly,
Blow, bonny breeze, my lover to me."

It was Annabell's voice, small and clear as a cricket singing alone, out of sight, in a corner. Dennis saw Uncle Simon Peter's gaze fix on them, the twinkle brighter than ever. He was looking at his face when the hand holding his went slack, and he felt Peter touching him on the shoulder.

"Come on, you two," he was saying. "It's time to go. Come. We must go and call Mamma."

Captain Roald Pieter Nielsen was buried at St. James' Parish Church beside his wife, Florence Annabell Nielsen, nee Ferguson, of the parish of St. James. The funeral was attended by no less a person than the Norwegian consul, who travelled all the way from Kingston for the occasion. Dennis was bitterly disappointed to discover that this worthy gentleman knew not a word of Norwegian, and was only some kind of honorary representative for the Norwegian government. To their parents' surprise, the three children took Uncle Simon Peter's death quite calmly, and only asked if they would please sing Psalm 139 at the service, because Maud said Aunt Flossie liked it. They showed no other interest in what went on, thinking rightly that all of the fuss amounted to what Uncle Simon Peter would have certainly described as nonsense. Mrs Edwards was of course at the funeral, and enjoyed herself very much.

The children missed him; how much only they could tell. They kept their remaining treasures very carefully ever after, even when they had grown up, and got married, and had children of their own. When first Peter, and then Dennis, reached the age of twenty-one, Annabell had two boars' heads cut off the silver chain and made into cuff links for them. But as the chain had been very long even when Aunt Flossie wore it, this made little difference. Annabell had her heart's desire, which was to go to school in Montego Bay and live at the house on Barnet Street, where she boarded with the Edwards'. About this time Miss French closed down her boarding house, so Peter went to live at Barnet Street too. A year later Dennis joined them, because old lawyer Foster died, and the Virgin Valley farm changed hands. Mr Ferguson rented a farm of his own over Tilston way, and the Fergusons' days at Somerton came to an end. Maud went to Tilston with Mr and Mrs Ferguson, and is buried in the churchyard there. She lived to a great age, and she was actually buried by Peter, who, to everyone's lasting astonishment, gave up his job with the Parish Council and went to train as a priest. His secret wish, still only a wish, is to serve as a priest in the navy, but he speaks of that only to Annabell and Dennis, on the rare occasions when he can catch his sister on her rounds as district nurse, or his brother on shore-leave from the banana boat *Aurora Borealis* on which he serves as second mate.